Tony Granger has a background in law, commerce and financial services and has been helping people create wealth and keep it, for over 15 years.

This retirement planning book is the first to deal with the *actual mechanics* and options available to people contemplating retirement or planning for it.

What to do when you get to retirement, which financial options are available, and when to take them; how to decide on the best course of action for your circumstances; selecting annuities, preserving your retirement capital; deciding on *how* to take your income in the most efficient way – these are all areas covered in this book, as well as many more.

There are useful strategies to eliminate the things you don't want and include the things you do; to maximise income and *increase* capital values after retirement; to stop the annuity providers from grabbing your capital; to allocate income and capital for dependants and heirs; to make the right choices and not make the wrong ones.

Tony Granger has been dealing with retirement issues such as these for nearly two decades, and lectures widely in the UK and abroad, as well as advising clients on pensions and retirement issues. He introduced the first open market option clearing house for pensions and annuities in the UK, as well as innovative new products, such as insuring your pension fund.

As a highly qualified independent financial adviser based in Harrogate, North Yorkshire, with The Independent Financial Partnership Limited, he advises clients and trains financial planners in all aspects of wealth creation and retirement planning. He is an international speaker on individual and corporate financial planning issues, and a past president of The Institute of Life and Pensions Advisers of South Africa, as well as a member of the Institute of Financial Planning and the Chartered Insurance Institute of the United Kingdom, amongst others.

Tony's many publications include guides to financial services for solicitors and accountants and a guide to venture capital trusts and enterprise investment schemes. His previous book is *Wealth Strategies for Your Business*, also published by Century (1996)

GW00599267

How to Finance Your Retirement

Over 100 powerful strategies to
increase your retirement income

TONY GRANGER

CENTURY
BUSINESS

This edition first published in the United Kingdom
in 1997 by Century Ltd
Random House, 20 Vauxhall Bridge Road,
London SW1V 2SA

Random House Australia (Pty) Limited
20 Alfred Street, Milsons Point, Sydney,
New South Wales 2061, Australia

Random House New Zealand Limited
18 Poland Road, Glenfield,
Auckland 10, New Zealand

Random House South Africa (Pty) Limited
Endulini, 5a Jubilee Road, Parktown 2193, South Africa

Random House UK Limited Reg. No. 954009

A CIP catalogue record for this book is available from the British Library

Papers used by Random House UK Limited are natural,
recyclable products made from wood grown in sustainable forests.
The manufacturing processes conform to the environmental
regulations of the country of origin.

ISBN 0 7126 7817 4

Typeset by MATS, Southend-on-Sea, Essex
Printed and bound in Great Britain by
Mackays of Chatham PLC, Chatham, Kent

Companies, institutions and other organizations wishing to make bulk
purchases of any business books published by Random House should
contact their local bookstore or Random House direct:
Special Sales Director
Random House, 20 Vauxhall Bridge Road,
London SW1V 2SA
Tel 0171 840 8470   Fax 0171 828 6681

Acknowledgements

I am most grateful to those who helped with the production of this important book which has taken many years of research, observation and determination to complete.

It comes at an interesting time – the newly-elected Labour government will no doubt give fresh impetus to the national retirement movement. To assist with event-tracking and scenario planning, I was pleased to have as a sounding board Ross Hyett, who was backed up by Brian Smyth, James O'Hare and, particularly, David McGee who critically examined the text. Working independently to give a fresh insight into the manuscript were the Winterthur team of John Moret, Angela Baskeyfield and Sandra Fulton who receive my heartfelt thanks for a job well done.

David Abbey and Billy Burrows provided immense technical back-up. Billy is pre-eminent in his field relating to annuities and a marvellous resource, as was Stuart Baylis from Annuity Direct.

Finally, to the person who has had the biggest job – the word processing and early production phases – Julie Backshall, who cheerfully helped me to beat the deadlines – congratulations on a job well done.

My appreciation to Elizabeth Hennessy of Random House/ Century for continuing to publish me.

This book has been made possible through the generous sponsorship of Wintherthur Life.

Objective:	To *focus* the reader on the money mechanics of retirement financial planning, beginning with adequate funding, through to the actual act of retirement and beyond, and its financial implications; to ensure a successful and stress-free life after work.
	To develop strategies to *implement* your retirement plan successfully, choosing the best options.
Retirement:	*'Seclusion; secluded place; condition of having retired from work'*
Retire:	*'(cricket) voluntarily terminate one's innings'* **The Oxford Illustrated Dictionary**
	'give up work, stop working, be pensioned off; be put out to grass' **The Concise Oxford Thesaurus**

Contents

Preface

The new Labour Government, elected in May 1997, has already begun to examine the State pension system and how it can best be reformed. Sweeping changes are expected in contribution rates to fund a new care pension to finance long-term care for the elderly. In addition, the basic State pension is to remain. However, those earning over £100 per week may have to pay into a second pension scheme, if not already in an occupational or personal scheme. This compulsory scheme (to be known as a 'stakeholder' pension) would encompass a new 'mutual fund' outside the control of private companies or life offices.

A possible restriction of the tax relief on pension contributions to the basic rate is widely expected, as well as some form of tax on lump sums from pension schemes. This could come in future budgets. It is also expected that the State Earnings Related Pension Scheme (SERPS) would remain as an option. Let us hope that 'things can only get better' (Labour campaign song) and that clear direction and adequate pension funding for all will result.

Over 60,000 people retire in the United Kingdom each month. That's an incredible 720,000 people per annum. Whilst this is good news for those who have properly planned their retirement according to their financial and personal needs, for many it is a time of great stress and a feeling of personal financial disaster when they realise that they do not have enough retirement capital from which to draw their retirement income.

Whilst there are a number of other books which deal with the psychological and the more human face of retirement, such as what to do with one's leisure time, how to eat more economically, and the prospects of moving to a smaller house, there has yet to be a publication which deals satisfactorily with the actual mechanics of retirement and its financial implications.

This book is aimed at those concerned retirees who wish to turn their retirement ideas into retirement reality.

Reality is a funny thing. If nothing else, it certainly focuses the mind on what has to be done in order to meet your personal financial planning objectives. Unfortunately, retirement planning does not start from the date when you lock your office door and ride off into the sunset; it starts when you begin your working life and only ends when you die. Ask anyone who has retired what they would have done differently, had they the opportunity, the means, and the insight to do so when they were most able. The answer is always translated into fear: a fear of living too long; a fear of outliving one's capital; a fear of the decreasing purchasing power of one's money; a fear of never having enough. These fears, which are applicable to 99% of the population, can be translated into retirement planning objectives, and from these can be developed strategies for you to become your own retirement planning expert.

There is much which can be done. If you want to learn how to increase your retirement income by 60% and more; how to protect your retirement funds from reverting back to the life assurers and pension funders on your death; how to protect your estate for your heirs; how to avoid losing your house should you have to go into long-term care and, above all, how to achieve a happy and contented retirement, then read on.

If you are fortunate enough to have attained your retirement objectives already, then perhaps some of the strategies outlined in this book will help you to keep more of what you have.

There is much to be said for having a total overview of the pensions and retirement planning market in the United Kingdom today. Those who have grown up with the system of State, occupational and personal pension funding and retirement planning have, over the years, tried to make a very complex situation even more complex. They don't just see a wood, they see the whole forest. As a retirement planning specialist coming to the UK from a more flexible and liberal retirement planning regime, I soon realised where the major gaps were for improvement. The first and most vital area was that of adequate information on which to base retirement planning decisions. For those with personal pensions and retirement annuities, the whole area of where to find out which insurers provided the best annuity rates and options was totally fragmented and without any cohesion. My in-depth research and analysis led to a collation of annuity rates on an industry-wide basis which, in turn, led to the establishment of the first annuity bureau as a clearing house for open market option annuities and the best rates for pensions in retirement.

Financial engineering with respect to increasing income in retirement has come a long way since then. It is now common for people with impaired lives or smokers to achieve higher annuity rates in retirement, as well as to manipulate their income requirements through drawing down pension income, whilst leaving a pension fund largely intact, without having to take out an annuity until legislatively forced to do so.

Having cracked the nut which would give retirees more income in retirement, other development work followed, which centred around the retention of capital for retirees and their heirs. It is now possible to pass your original retirement fund intact to your spouse or other heirs, without losing it to the life office or pension provider which assisted you with the build-up of your retirement funding over your working lifetime.

The strategies in this book will guide you through the complex maze of legislation, regulation and available information, thus enabling you to make crisp and accurate financial planning decisions to give you peace of mind for your financial future.

This book is aimed at the financial heart of retirement planning. It concentrates on the money mechanics of retirement, ranging from proper pension funding and investments, through to the actual act of retirement and its financial implications. The book then goes further by incorporating aspects of long-term care and estate planning – aspects which naturally follow retirement planning.

These powerful retirement strategies will not only show you how to save money for the future, but also how to create wealth. Above all they will create the correct focus through giving a step-by-step approach, whatever your personal circumstances or future requirements will be.

The book is based on my understanding of current tax law and relevant legislation at the time of writing. The implication of some of the strategies may require the reader to seek further professional advice, which should be considered, in any event, prior to the implementation of any strategies. Where investments are mentioned, the reader's attention is drawn to the fact that values may fluctuate up and down and that past performance is no guarantee of future success. Where loans are secured against property, there is always the risk of losing the property if loan payments are not maintained. Carefully consider your personal circumstances before implementing any strategies as the author cannot be held responsible for any acts, errors or omissions (E & OE).

In addition, the views contained in this book are those of the author alone and in *no way* reflect those of the sponsor, Wintherthur Life.

Figures used in calculations throughout the text refer to the 1997/98 tax year.

Tony Granger
Harrogate, August 1997

Abbreviations

AIM	Alternative Investment Market
AVC	Additional Voluntary Contribution to the initial pension scheme
CGT	Capital Gains Tax
DSS	Department of Social Security
EIS	Enterprise Investment Scheme
EPP	Executive Pension Plan
ESOT	Employee Share Owner Trust
EZT	Enterprise Zone Trust
FS	Final Salary
FSAVC	Free Standing Additional Voluntary Contribution to an independent pension provider
FT-SE	Financial Times-Stock Exchange
FURBS	Funded Unapproved Retirement Benefit Scheme
GAD	Government Actuaries Department
GMP	Guaranteed Minimum Pension
GPPP	Group Personal Pension Plan
IA	Immediate Annuity
N	Figure denoting years of service in an occupational pension scheme
NI(C)	National Insurance (Contributions)
OEICS	Open Ended Investment Company Schemes
OMO	Open Market Option
OPM	Other People's Money
P	Pension factor used to work out the pension payable
PAYE	Pay As You Earn income tax collection from employer
PEP	Personal Equity Plan
PHI	Permanent Health Insurance
PIBS	Permanent Interest Bearing Shares
PLA	Purchased Life Annuity
PPP	Personal Pension Plan
PRP	Profit Related Pay
PSO	Pensions Schemes Office
RPI	Retail Price Index (measures inflation)
SERPS	State Earnings Related Pension Scheme
SIPP	Self-invested Personal Pension Plan
SSAS	Small Self-Administered Scheme

TESSA   Tax Exempt Special Savings Account
VCT   Venture Capital Trust
VPA   Voluntary Purchase Annuity

The Retirement Process
The retirement process diagram shows the lifetime of accumulation of pension and savings, leading to normal retirement date and the expectation of capital and income.

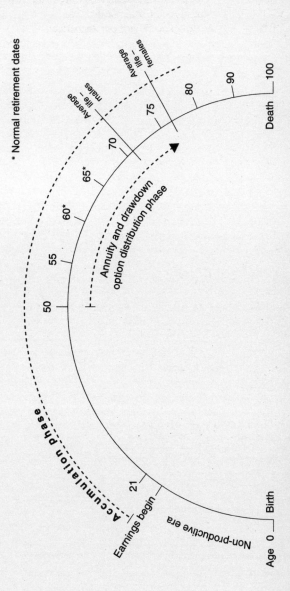

* Normal retirement dates

Accumulation phase

Annuity and drawdown
option distribution phase

Average
life –
females

Average
life –
males

50   55   60*   65*   70   75   80   90   100

Earnings begin

21

Age 0   Birth

Non-productive era

Death

The Retirement Financing Process

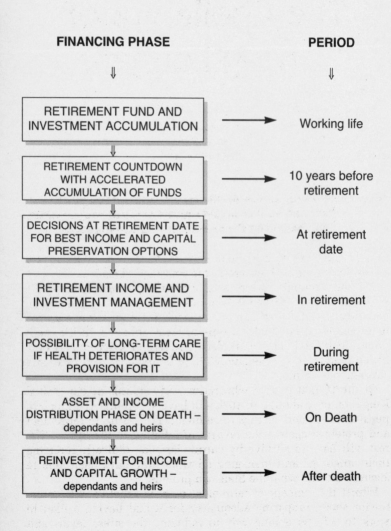

FINANCING PHASE

⇓

PERIOD

⇓

RETIREMENT FUND AND INVESTMENT ACCUMULATION	Working life
RETIREMENT COUNTDOWN WITH ACCELERATED ACCUMULATION OF FUNDS	10 years before retirement
DECISIONS AT RETIREMENT DATE FOR BEST INCOME AND CAPITAL PRESERVATION OPTIONS	At retirement date
RETIREMENT INCOME AND INVESTMENT MANAGEMENT	In retirement
POSSIBILITY OF LONG-TERM CARE IF HEALTH DETERIORATES AND PROVISION FOR IT	During retirement
ASSET AND INCOME DISTRIBUTION PHASE ON DEATH – dependants and heirs	On Death
REINVESTMENT FOR INCOME AND CAPITAL GROWTH – dependants and heirs	After death

CHAPTER 1

The Challenge of Living Longer

Old age is like everything else.
To make a success of it, you've got
to start young.'
Fred Astaire

Objective: How to prepare for life for retirement, taking into account your changing circumstances as you get older, and beginning the retirement countdown process

Preparing for life in retirement is much the same as preparing for anything. You must have realisable goals and objectives.

The mere thought of the word 'retirement' usually produces a negative reaction in people's minds: retirement is a time when being truly useful ceases; it is a time when income from employment ceases; it is usually a time of great upheaval in life, both domestically and in the workplace. The reason is that most people haven't managed to save enough in order to enjoy a peaceful and stress-free retirement.

Of the 60,000 people who retire every month in the United Kingdom, only about 5 to 10% will have accumulated enough in pension funds and savings to be financially secure in retirement and protected against the ravages of inflation in the future. The rest will have to survive by cutting corners, radically reducing their outgoings and managing on what they have been able to accumulate and what the State can provide.

Whilst the concept of retirement may be negative and stressful for some, preparing adequately for it and having a plan to work to will go a long way to reducing the stress levels and making the retirement years an enjoyable prospect.

It is a fact of modern life that more and more people are thinking of retiring earlier and, in fact, are doing so. Therefore their accumulated funds must provide for a longer period of retirement. In addition, it is also a fact that people are living longer due to advanced medical techniques, better diet and eating habits and modern-day inventions which have made life easier. At the turn of the century, the average life expectancy of a male was only 49 years. For a female, it was 52. In the late 1990s, the average life expectancy for a male is 73 years and that for a female is 77 years. In less than a span of 100 years, life expectancy has gone up by nearly 50%. The challenge of living longer can also be translated into the challenge of outliving your accumulated savings and pension plans as life expectancy increases. You will be *retired* for five times *longer* than your grandfather was, on average. 'Risk' in the twentieth century has been connected with the possibility of losing your money, whereas 'risk' in the twenty-first century will be outliving your money.

This challenge can only be met by preparing adequately for retirement and the fact that you may spend more of your life not working than you have spent in the workplace.

The UK population as a whole is also ageing, mainly due to a relatively static population. The *average* age of our population will be 37 by the year 2000 and by 2010 it will be 40! On average, the bulk of the population is closer to retirement age than starting out on the first rungs of the work ladder. In fact, 20% of the entire population (over 10 million people) are retired – a factor which is set to accelerate in future years.

Some – about 10% – have retired 'well' financially, whereas 30% of retired people are living at subsistence levels or below. Ill-health in declining years is a major problem, affecting over 50% of the retired population, as one would expect.

STRATEGY 1
Be prepared to step up your retirement funding programme as much as possible

---

For younger people, as well as people with families or children at school and university, their major priority is for immediate lifestyle planning as opposed to longer-term retirement planning.

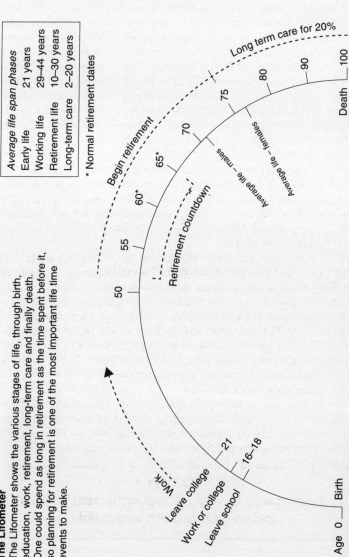

The Lifometer
The Lifometer shows the various stages of life, through birth, education, work, retirement, long-term care and finally death. One could spend as long in retirement as the time spent before it, so planning for retirement is one of the most important life time events to make.

Average life span phases
Early life   21 years
Working life   29–44 years
Retirement life 10–30 years
Long-term care   2–20 years

* Normal retirement dates

Long term care for 20%

Begin retirement

Average life – females

Average life – males

Retirement countdown

Work

Leave college

Work or college

Leave school

100
90
80
75
70
65*
60*
55
50
21
16–18
Death

Age 0   Birth

One wakes up to the adequacy or otherwise of one's own retirement planning endeavours perhaps only 10 or 15 years before retirement, and for the majority of people this only happens within five years of retirement. Thus, whilst it makes sense to begin saving for retirement as early as possible, the vast bulk of retirement funding will, in all likelihood, occur in the years immediately preceding retirement. Earlier on in one's working life, for most households, after paying off the mortgage and paying for household necessities, there is precious little left over to spend on retirement fund accumulation. Yet, as you get older and earnings increase, your personal retirement programme should be stepped up significantly.

To prepare adequately for the challenge of retirement, you must remove two conditioned thought processes from your thinking.

STRATEGY 2
Do not wholly depend on the State or employer for your retirement security – prepare mentally how to take up the challenge

---

There are two common beliefs.

The first is that the State will provide for you in retirement and until you die. It will also provide for your family and dependants should you no longer be around to support them.

The second is that your employer will adequately provide for you and you need do nothing more than merely work each day and remain there until you retire from age 50 to 65.

These beliefs are, unfortunately, fundamentally flawed. First, the Conservative government prior to May 1987, publicly announced on numerous occasions, and put into action, a winding-down of its own State Earnings Related Pension Scheme (SERPS). That government also made it quite clear that it would not be in a position to provide adequate old age pensions forever. A new initiative, aimed at the privatisation of the State pensions sector, was announced in March 1997. However, the new Labour government, elected in May 1997, will not privatise the State pension but is committed to enhancing it – a massive funding priority. (See strategy 74.)

In fact, there is no old age pension scheme in the United Kingdom. There is no actuarially-defined government fund where your National Insurance contributions are invested on your behalf and from which you may draw a retirement income. What happens is, quite simply, that those who are working pay National Insurance contributions in on the Friday, and those who are in retirement draw out the pension benefits from the same scheme on the Monday.

As fewer and fewer people remain in the workplace, and more and more people retire, the cost of providing State old age pensions is going to escalate. It is a fair estimation that in 25 years' time, individual National Insurance contributions will have doubled, if not quadrupled, for the same, or less, amount of pension to be drawn in the future.

To illustrate this, in 1997, 2.2 workers support one person who is a pensioner. In the year 2020, it is estimated that 1.8 working people will support 1 person who is a pensioner. The government is on record as saying that it expects the population to be responsible for its own retirement funding plans. Don't expect any real help from the State. The current old age pension is barely in excess of £60 a week, and it is not really going to get any better. A recent study in Italy concluded that funding pensions for its population would consume 70% of the country's gross domestic product – and the figure is over 100% for France and Germany. The message is frighteningly similar for the UK, but is not as high, due to previous measures undertaken by the government to reduce the future cost of State schemes. This is good news for workers, but not for pensioners.

The second most unfortunate mistake made by people preparing for retirement is that they rely on their employers in effect to guess how much they, the employees, will require in retirement and for their employers to provide for them adequately. Whilst there are some superb company and other business pension schemes around for employees, in the main these are few and far between, and are highly unlikely to provide satisfactory financial security in retirement. Yet, the mere fact that they are in an employer's pension scheme, may seem to the employees to be adequate. Naturally, schemes differ from employer to employer, yet even the very best employer final salary scheme cannot legally give you a pension of more than two-thirds of your final salary. That two-thirds is usually accumulated with 40 years of unbroken service. If you do not wish to see a significant fall in living standards, then *you* have to make up the difference.

STRATEGY 3
Become a lifestyle planner – learn how to apportion your disposable income

---

Instead of merely telling you about retirement planning as a concept, let us begin by examining the concept of *lifestyle planning* and approach this in a sensible way which is easy to follow. This concept is developed around what is known as the *four-pillar philosophy* – that is, you will require different planning objectives depending upon your personal or expected circumstances at any particular time.

The four-pillar philosophy in action

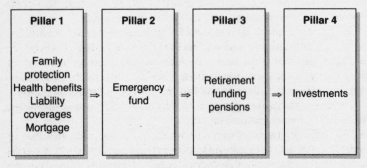

A number of examples will illustrate how the four-pillar philosophy works for any combination of circumstances. It applies on the basis of the net disposable income available to cover certain aspects of lifestyle planning. Each of the pillars and their applications must be approached in a logical order. If one aspect does not apply, then you move on to the next one in order to distribute your disposable income in the most efficient method in respect of personal financial planning.

Our first example is that of Jeff and Donna, a married couple who have two minor children, a mortgage and credit card liabilities. Because both parents work, their net disposable income is, say, £500 per month. This is the amount which they have to spend *after* living expenses.

Following our *four-pillar philosophy*, in financial planning terms, the family should first ensure: that there is adequate family protection through life assurance and critical illness cover; that income is protected through permanent health insurance (PHI) and that current liabilities are catered for – pillar 1.

Any further disposable income should be diverted to an accessible deposit account for emergencies (at least three months' income). This is the second pillar in the process. Only then should Jeff and Donna consider pension funding as the third step in the process; any income left over could then be allocated to the fourth pillar – investments.

The four-pillar philosophy works. It works because it prioritises financial planning needs according to your circumstances. It would be irresponsible for the £500 available to be invested in a PEP or unit trust if no family protection through life assurance was in place.

Take the example of Anna, a widow aged 82. She has no need for life cover; requires an emergency fund; is already retired, and will therefore focus on making investments for income or capital growth – but she requires an emergency fund first.

On the other hand, Bob is aged 55 and married to Carol, age 51. He has no dependants and wishes to retire at age 60. Bob will have less of a need for life cover – he has sufficient assets to cover an emergency fund and his primary focus will be to maximise pension funding, following by building an investment portfolio.

Use this four-pillar process to allocate your own resources, according to your circumstances.

Whilst totally correct from a financial planning point of view, in reality the situation of having to provide for current lifestyle needs means that there is usually very little left over to provide adequate funds for longer-term objectives, such as retirement. This often means that retirement funding is a poor cousin to other financial commitments for probably over two-thirds of one's working life.

It is a well-known fact that those with children in fee paying education cannot afford to fund for both school or college fees *and* retirement at the same time. Where resources are finite, choices are made along the lines of personal priorities.

STRATEGY 4
Look at insurance cover now, for flexibility later

Most people will not be anywhere near funding for retirement at the desired levels. You may consider the final objective of

satisfactorily financing your retirement as being out of reach. You
may do something towards it, but not reach 100% of your target –
nor can you hope to. What should you do about this? Well, if
retirement funding is going to be adequate, then you have to give
yourself the chance of having *absolute flexibility to consider every
option* at retirement.

This strategy creates an opportunity for most people early on in
the lifestyle planning process. The first pillar concerned family
protection and adequate life assurance cover. Taking out a whole
of life policy at any age *before* retirement is going to be cheaper
than at retirement.

Why talk about life assurance when retirement planning is the
issue?

Because, if you are able to do so, this will be the smartest move
you will ever make. It will *guarantee* you an increase in your
retirement income of up to 60% – just by giving you the option of
taking an annuity for a single life *without* a guarantee. You do this
by insuring the amount of your retirement fund value. This frees
up your thinking – and, incidentally, 60% more income can
equate to a pension fund worth hundreds of thousands of pounds
which you did not have to save for!

The secret is to increase your life insurance significantly –
always whole of life or 50-year term policies from age 45 – to have
a sum assured of your eventual proposed pension fund value. It
helps *earlier on* for family protection and *later on* allows secure
and safe option selection at retirement.

Apart from the feeling that your retirement funds will be fully protected on your death, and the flexibility given to you to elect the highest level of income, you also have the personal choice whether to
continue with your protection plan in retirement or not. Remember,
the difference between the joint and survivor guaranteed annuity rate
offered to yourself when you retire (this will pay out a pension for
both you and your spouse for your lifetimes) and *the best open market option rate* available, which is a single life with no guarantee, in
the marketplace could be as much as 60% more income. Depending
on where you built up your initial pension funds, the amount could
be in excess of 100% more income from the date of retirement. This
figure comes from comparing the lowest rate joint and survivor
annuity, with guarantees for 5 years and escalating by 3% to the best
open market option single life annuity with no guarantee.

Chapter 9 discusses these strategies in more detail including a
table of likely costs, whilst Chapter 6 shows the different rates.

Most people work, and then they retire. Some prepare for that event adequately. Others do not. The pressure on you to prepare for eventual retirement is more remote the younger you are. The older you become, the greater is the pressure to make proper preparations for retirement with adequate planning. It is therefore *most important* that, as part of the retirement planning process, a structured approach is in place within, say, 10 to 15 years of retirement. This is known as the 'Retirement Countdown Planning Process'.

STRATEGY 5
Learn how the retirement countdown planning process will benefit you and give a clear overview of your position at any time

---

The following personal financial plan will best illustrate how you can construct a retirement countdown chart for yourself:

RETIREMENT COUNTDOWN EVENT CHART TO AGE 65

The chart assumes a married couple, the male aged 50 now and the female aged 40. Their strategy is to consider, year by year, their investments and outgoings and when maturities such as endowments and pension plans will take place. This process gives a visual overview of what has to be done over the years to retirement. Draw up your own chart using this format.

Year	Age a	Age b	Strategy	Invest	Outgoings
1997	50	40	Boost pension. PEPS		
1998	51	41	Boost pension. PEPS		
1999	52	42	Boost pension. PEPS		
2000	53	43	Boost pension. PEPS		
2001	54	44	Boost pension. PEPS		
2002	55	45	Boost pension. PEPS		
2003	56	46	Boost pension. PEPS		
2004	57	47	Boost pension. PEPS		
2005	58	48	Boost pension. PEPS		
			Mortgage paid off		
			Endowment matures		

Year	Age a	Age b	Strategy	Invest	Outgoings
2006	59	49	Boost pension. PEPS		
2007	60	50	Endowment matures		
			Boost pension. PEPS		
2008	61	51	Boost pension. PEPS		
2009	62	52	Term cover ends		
			Boost pension. PEPS		
2010	63	53	Boost pension. PEPS		
2011	64	54	Boost pension		
			Purchase new car		
2012	65	55	Normal retirement date		
			Personal pension		
			fund matures		
2013	66	56	Endowment matures:		
2014	67	57			

When you actually enter into the retirement countdown process will indicate the breadth of planning options available to you.

Our second example shows a much tighter retirement countdown planning process where the husband, in this case, is aged 60 wishing to retire at age 65 and his spouse is aged 55 wishing to retire at age 60.

RETIREMENT COUNTDOWN PROGRAMME TO AGE 65

Year	Age a	Age b	
1997	60	55	} Maximise pension funding and
1998	61	56	} investments to age 65
1999	62	57	
2000	63	58	
2001	64	59	Endowment matures £30,000
2002	65	60	Pension fund matures £160,000
2003	66	61	Pay off mortgage from lump sum £40,000
2004	67	62	Term cover ends

In order to reach their retirement planning objectives, the first couple have a much longer retirement countdown plan in place which does not have as much impact on their disposable income as does the second couple's. The second couple may need to increase their funding at much higher levels.

STRATEGY 6
Complete your own retirement countdown plan

Using the example given above, as part of your preparation, complete your own retirement countdown plan. Once you have completed it, you will then have a bird's-eye picture of what your plan will look like visually so that you can time your pension and investment funding towards certain defined dates.

As it is important to obtain up-to-date values of your various investments, endowment policies, personal equity plans, shares and others, you may wish to write and request the values from the product provider yourself, or you may wish to ask your financial adviser to construct your initial plan for you from which you can work. Include every aspect of your future lifestyle planning – for example, possibly selling a house at age 60 to move to a smaller property, thus extinguishing your mortgage; the dates at which you expect investments to mature, or need replacing; the dates at which life insurance and other benefits may cease; various options you might have to make at certain dates, as well as decisions.

STRATEGY 7
Develop your lifetime blueprint plan for success

This plan will then become your *blueprint* for the rundown towards retirement. Various additional options and other strategies will be discussed in the coming chapters to keep you on track.

The planning process continues for the whole of your lifetime. Whilst most people are more concerned with planning up until the date of retirement, a significant amount of post-retirement planning will also be undertaken as lifestyle circumstances change. The cross-over from retirement planning into retirement itself, and then into possible long-term care, are all factors which must be weighed in the preparation process. Obviously the longer you have to plan adequately for retirement, the better.

If you are up against the wire and absolutely dreading the onset of your retirement because you feel you will be financially insecure, then it is still not too late to do something about it, however small. The strategies which have already been discussed and those which will be found in coming chapters, will show you how to make the best of your present and future situation. More than that, they will indicate options to you which you probably did not know existed and assist you in deciding which option will be best for your own circumstances. The next major step which needs to be undertaken in respect of financing your retirement, is to determine what your main objectives for retirement are going to be and how best to reach them.

Key points summary

- Due to increasing levels of life expectancy, people will not only live longer, but will also be retired for longer.
- The general trend is towards earlier retirement with a longer period spent in retirement.
- Most people fear outliving their capital and thus the means to produce increasing income.
- Initial preparation strategies are given for more flexible options at retirement.
- A critical path analysis is given for lifestyle planning with changing circumstances and disposable income allocation.
- Preparing the retirement countdown programme.
- Meeting the challenge of living as long as your money.

Action plan

1. Decide how many years you will most likely spend in retirement: _____
2. How much money do you have *left over* each month? _____
3. **Prioritise your financial resources *now*.**

   Family protection _____   Emergency fund   _____
   Health benefits   _____   Retirement funding and
                                pensions   _____
   Liabilities   _____   Investments   _____
   Other   _____

4. Construct your own retirement countdown plan chart or matrix including dates of maturities of pensions and investments.
5. Level of life cover now: _____

CHAPTER 2

Setting Your Retirement Goals

Be like a postage stamp – stick to one thing until you get there.
Margaret Carty

Objective: Formulating your major definitive purpose in respect of financing your retirement and setting your action plans and objectives

There used to be two certainties in life – death and taxes. I believe there are actually three: one can add 'retirement' to the list.

Whilst it is impossible to cheat death, marginally possible to cheat the tax man, unless you die before you retire it is impossible to cheat yourself out of retirement. Granted, there are a few workaholics around, who will soldier on to the bitter end, but these are few and far between. At some stage, at the end of your working life, you will want to put your feet up and take it easy in the full knowledge that you have worked for your money, and now your money must work for you.

Generally speaking, we have different objectives for different situations. If I were to ask you what your main objective is in life, you might say: 'To be happy', 'To be secure financially', 'To build lasting relationships with loved ones', or, more specifically: 'To save up enough money to buy a house', 'To change jobs for better prospects', 'To be able to live life to the full without any worries'.

Most of us go through life without any defined and focused objectives. We have visions of things we would like to do and, as our circumstances change, so does our outlook for the future. If your vision is that you wish to enjoy a happy and contented retirement without any financial stress, then your *focus* must be on what you need to do in order to achieve this objective.

STRATEGY 8
Decide on your vision for the future. Focus on what you need to do to get there

---

If retirement is one of the inevitabilities of life, then, in financial planning terms, it should provide a long-term primary focus for achievement. The definitive purpose of this book is to provide the most effective means of financing your retirement and then to deal with the actual mechanics of the retirement process, so that you are placed in the best position possible to exercise the various strategies and options available to you, taking your own circumstances into account.

If your major purpose is to enjoy a happy and financially secure retirement, the underlying focus of our endeavours is how to reach that goal and by what means.

How big should your retirement fund be? How much is enough? Can you afford to pay the price to get there? What needs to be done to achieve this objective, and do you have the determination to do it?

STRATEGY 9
Identify your likely target retirement fund amount

No one ever said it was going to be easy. The easy option is to do nothing. If you take the easy option, you will surely fail in your objective. It is only by concentrating your mind and your energies on the task in hand, that all things become possible. Not only must you prepare the way, you must also have a plan to put into practice, however short or long-term. You must identify your targets. In this case, your target retirement fund amount needs to be ascertained, broken down into bite-sized chunks and attacked with vigour.

How does one work out what a likely retirement fund should be? This question naturally depends on how much income, as well as capital, you will need from your retirement date.

STRATEGY 10
Decide on your retirement date and how much income you want in retirement

It is important to establish your normal retirement date. Having settled on that (if it is not decided for you, which may well be the case if you are an employee in an employer's pension fund), you have to decide the level of income you wish to have in retirement. If you want your standard of living to remain constant, you will need 100% of your final salary to be the same as your retirement income – possibly increasing with inflation. If, however, you feel that you can get by with less, as your personal circumstances will be less financially exacting, you can choose an amount of, say, two-thirds of your final salary, or maybe even half the amount. By law, an approved pension fund, through its restrictive funding practices, will give you a pension of only two-thirds of your final salary.

This means that your retirement income is probably going to be funded not only through pension provision, but also through investments which will provide you with income and capital later on in life.

STRATEGY 11
Decide which liabilities to eliminate by retirement

From your retirement countdown chart, you will know what liabilities you will wish to eliminate by your retirement. For example, you may not have paid off your mortgage and may wish to do so at that date. If you do not have a mortgage repayment vehicle in place, you may wish to use a part of your tax-free lump sum which accrues from your pension scheme, or perhaps from the encashment of one of your investments.

There are other factors which have to be taken into account – for example, the amount of the State old age pension to which you are entitled; the fact that you may live in a household where both partners are able to contribute to their own pension funding and therefore hope to enjoy joint incomes in retirement; the ages when you begin the funding process in earnest; the length of time you have to build up a meaningful fund for retirement; the possibility that future governments may wish to tax your pension fund investment income, thereby effectively reducing your capital for retirement.

You also have to take a view of what the average rate of inflation is going to be over the period through which you will be investing, and take that into account, as well as the effect of salary increases until retirement.

STRATEGY 12

Decide on the future rate of inflation as well as future income increases to get your future income requirement at retirement

---

In broad calculation terms, if you wish to retire on the income you are presently enjoying, and then to adjust that for inflation, as well as salary increases, you would end up with an income amount which shows a greater future value at retirement date.

Let us assume, by way of an example, that you are presently earning £30,000 per annum. You are aged 40 and you wish to retire at age 65. In your opinion, you believe that inflation will average, say, 6% per annum over the next 25 years and you can expect a salary increase of approximately 4% per annum over the same period.

You would then expect to receive, as a final salary from your employment or enterprise endeavours at age 65, approximately £80,000. If you were earning £15,000 a year now, then the final salary at age 65 is £41,500.

STRATEGY 13

Work out how much your target fund should be at retirement date

---

To ascertain the amount of investment and pension funds required at age 65, you should now take a view on how investments will perform over the next 25 years. On average, this will probably be between 5 and 10% on an annual compound basis, and we can take an average of, say, 8% for this exercise.

We are now in a position to work out the total amount of investment and pension funds which you will require at age 65 in order to produce your target income. There is one final calculation which needs to be made, and that is to estimate the percentage of income which can be earned, either as interest or annuity from your investments and pension funds. In this case we shall assume 10% per annum.

As the above-mentioned process is rather taxing for the average investor, the matrix reproduced below can be used as a handy ready-reckoner.

Find out where your present salary is in the left-hand column, note your years to retirement, and find the figure where the two columns meet. This will give you the value of your projected retirement fund, taking into account the above factors.

Target fund at 100%

Earnings per year	Years to retirement							
	1	5	10	15	20	25	30	35
£100,000	£1,040,000	£1,216,653	£1,480,244	£1,800,944	£2,191,123	£2,665,836	£3,243,398	£3,946,089
£80,000	£832,000	£973,322	£1,184,195	£1,440,755	£1,752,899	£2,132,669	£2,594,718	£3,156,871
£60,000	£624,000	£729,992	£888,147	£1,080,566	£1,314,674	£1,599,502	£1,946,039	£2,367,653
£40,000	£416,000	£486,661	£592,098	£720,377	£876,449	£1,066,335	£1,297,359	£1,578,436
£35,000	£364,000	£425,829	£518,085	£630,330	£766,893	£933,043	£1,135,189	£1,381,131
£30,000	£312,000	£364,996	£444,073	£540,283	£657,337	£799,751	£973,019	£1,183,827
£25,000	£260,000	£304,163	£370,061	£450,236	£547,781	£666,459	£810,849	£986,522
£20,000	£208,000	£243,331	£296,049	£360,189	£438,225	£533,167	£648,680	£789,218
£15,000	£156,000	£182,498	£222,037	£270,142	£328,668	£399,875	£486,510	£591,913
£10,000	£104,000	£121,665	£148,024	£180,094	£219,112	£266,584	£324,340	£394,609
£5,000	£52,000	£60,833	£74,012	£90,047	£109,556	£133,292	£162,170	£197,304

Assumptions: earnings growth 4% p.a., annuity % used 10%.
For a target fund of ⅔, merely take ⅔ of the figure shown.
For a target fund of 50%, take half of the figure shown.

Example 1
Assume Tom Smith currently enjoys an income of £30,000 and is presently aged 40. As he has 25 years to go to retirement, the estimated fund required is £799,751 if he wants to retire on 100% of salary at that time.

Example 2
Assume Geraldine Smith is aged 55 and receives a salary of
£15,000. Again, find the figure at the intersection of Geraldine's
salary and years to retirement of 10 years. In this case, the figure
is £222,037 for 100% of salary at that time. This is the fund value
required to give the target income of 100%. For 50% target
income, merely divide the above amount by two (£111,018).

Write in your target investment fund for retirement in this box.

£

You will now have a realistic expectation of how much you need
to fund for in order to achieve adequate finance for your
retirement free of financial worries. Your next objective will be to
work out how much you must put aside each month in order to
meet your retirement investment fund objectives.

STRATEGY 14
**Work out how much to save each month to meet your
overall investment fund objectives**

Finding the monthly investment amount

The following table will help you with your calculations.

*Amount required to produce £10,000 worth of funds at any
given period to retirement date*

Years to retirement	Monthly premium	Years to retirement	Monthly premium
1	£798.0	18	£17.5
2	£380.0	19	£15.5
3	£241.0	20	£14.0
4	£172.0	21	£12.5
5	£130.0	22	£11.0
6	£103.0	23	£10.0
7	£84.0	24	£9.0

Years to retirement	Monthly premium	Years to retirement	Monthly premium
8	£69.5	25	£8.0
9	£58.5	26	£7.5
10	£50.0	27	£6.5
11	£43.0	28	£6.0
12	£37.0	29	£5.5
13	£32.5	30	£5.0
14	£28.5	31	£4.5
15	£25.0	32	£4.0
16	£22.0	33	£3.7
17	£19.5	34	£3.3

Assumption: 10% growth net of all charges and any taxes

On the table find the number of years to your retirement and read off the monthly premium that will yield £10,000 on retirement.

Decide on a total target fund (see p. 18). Divide this by 10,000 and multiply the resulting figure by the monthly premium you have found on the above table. The result will be the amount you will need to save each month on a compound interest basis, in order to meet your target.

You can do this exercise for yourself by merely inserting the figures in the boxes below.

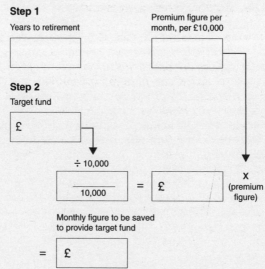

Example

Jack has 19 years to go to retirement. His eventual target fund is £200,000.

At 19 years, the monthly figure per £10,000 is £15.50.

£200,000 ÷ £10,000 = 20

20 × £15.50 = *£310*

So, if Jack has 19 years to go to retirement, and requires a fund amount of £200,000, he must save £310 per month.

Whilst the bulk of your investment funding will probably be into a pension scheme, in some cases you may not qualify to make pension payments, or pension contributions will not provide you with the desired amount, and you may need to make savings into a Personal Equity Plan, unit trust, investment trust or other capital growth investment vehicle.

STRATEGY 15
For complete accuracy, use a qualified retirement planner to help you

---

Whilst the above calculations are designed to assist you along your retirement journey, they may not be completely accurate for your purposes. If you feel that this is the case, please contact your financial adviser who will take your exact circumstances into account in making the calculations for you.

Doing this exercise can often be a frightening experience for retirement planning investors who may have left it a bit late. The reality is that, even if this is the case, *it is never too late to start with your investment plan*. You may not fully achieve your objectives, but at least you will have done something to finance your retirement plans.

STRATEGY 16
Begin the funding process as soon as possible, to avoid the cost of delay

---

The main factor to be borne in mind with any long-term investment planning is that, the sooner you can begin, the lighter will be your monthly investment funding load. Let us consider the cost of delay, translated into loss of final benefits.

By examining the table below, you will see the impact at various ages on eventual benefit, through delaying by only one year the beginning of your investment funding plan.

COST OF DELAY – EVENTUAL FUND LOST BY DELAYING FURTHER
PROVISION BY ONLY ONE YEAR

Delay period	% loss of benefit – Retire age 65
Age 21-22	15%
Age 31-32	15%
Age 41-42	16%
Age 51-52	18%
Age 61-62	38%

As you can see, by merely delaying the beginning of the funding of your investment plan by one year, at various periods in your life, a significant negative impact is made on your eventual fund value. The impact is much higher, the longer you delay.

You have now laid the groundwork for your retirement requirements, and the next chapter will show you, on a step-by-step basis, how to undertake retirement funding in the most tax-efficient and least costly way.

Key points summary

- Choosing your main definitive purpose in financial planning.
- How to become your own financial expert in working out the size of fund you need to accumulate for retirement and the monthly amounts needed to fund it.
- The cost of delay by only one year in beginning the process.

- Completion of the first phase of preparation for the retirement journey.

Action plan

1. Define your major objectives. These are:
    1.1 I wish to retire at age: _____
    1.2 I wish to retire on an income of __% of my salary or earnings.
    1.3 I will require a target retirement fund of £_____
    1.4 I can invest £_____ per month towards my objectives.
2. I will become my own financial expert ❏ or I will seek retirement advice ❏

CHAPTER 3

How to Build Your Own Super-charged Retirement Fund

The trouble with life in the fast lane is that you get to the other end in an awful hurry.
John Jensen
Begin with the end in mind.
The 7 Habits of Highly Effective People, Stephen Covey

Objective: Funding strategies to build a cost-effective retirement fund making use of available tax allowances

The previous two chapters dealt with the 'why?' behind the process or concept of retirement planning. This chapter will take you through the possibilities – or the 'how?' – of funding for your retirement plans, using the most tax-efficient methods available. The different kinds of pension plans and structures range from the easy-to-understand to the more complicated, depending upon your preferences and your position in the workplace. It is true to say that greater opportunities for higher levels of funding are available to, for example, directors of companies, as opposed to employees, or the self-employed. Each type of retirement plan structure has different rules attached in respect of the size of contributions which may be legally made, and there are alternatives available for those who are already at maximum funding limits and are looking for other retirement funding vehicles.

There are, broadly speaking, three categories for funding for those in employment and the self-employed:

- Employees
- Directors
- Self-employed and partners

and one category for those with:

- non-earned income

The following quick reference guide to funding strategies for various categories should help to guide you through this chapter.

Employees	Strategies 18 to 29 and 40
Directors	Strategies 30 to 32
Self-employed	Strategies 33 to 39
Partners	Strategies 41 to 45
Non-earners	Strategy 46
The State	Strategies 47 to 48
Charges and Performance	Strategies 49 to 52

To build a super-charged retirement fund requires careful planning, taking into account your personal circumstances, the structure of your employee benefits if you are a director or employee, and the size and source of your income flow if you are a partner or self-employed. One also needs to take into account the proposed investment to be made, and the charging structure associated with this investment. Whilst a lot has been said to warn against taking too much notice of past investment performance when determining what your future investment possibilities are, it is also natural that one should concentrate on proven investment managers who can deliver real returns against inflation.

STRATEGY 17
Be prepared to switch to better investment managers

If possible, one should look to retirement plans where, if the longer-term investment performance is lacking, you would not be penalised by switching to another investment manager who can deliver a solid high-level investment performance. Indeed, the astute management and monitoring of your investments is one of the areas which could deliver a higher-value and super-charged retirement fund, as opposed to a mediocre performer. In fact, a 1% loss of investment performance over a 20-year period can equate to an eventual fund deficit of up to 18%. It is therefore important to aim for the utmost in investment performance in order to boost your eventual fund value.

IF YOU ARE AN EMPLOYEE

Employees in businesses are likely to be in one of the following positions:

- In their employer's final salary or money purchase occupational pension scheme.
- A member of a group personal pension scheme sponsored by the employer.
- Not in any pension arrangement and having to make their own arrangements.

If you are an employee with a final salary scheme

Employees who are members of a final salary scheme will probably, on average, be better off than employees obtaining pension benefits elsewhere. A final salary scheme is one which pays out a pension to the employee, which is based on the amount of his or her final salary, or an average of, say, the last three years' worth of salary prior to retirement date.

STRATEGY 18
**Ascertain what your maximum pension benefits are
likely to be at retirement**

Employer occupational pension schemes account for more than
50% of the working population. Pension benefits must be paid on
retirement between the ages of 50 and 75. These benefits cannot
exceed the maximum permitted, which is calculated taking into
account the employee's final remuneration and length of service
with that employer, plus retained benefits.

The *maximum pension benefits* are:

 i) Pre-1987 – ⅔ × final remuneration after 10 years' service (no
    earnings cap).
ii) Post-1987 – ⅔ × final remuneration after 20 years' service
    (earnings cap applies).

Fractions apply for lesser periods.

One cannot have a pension of more than ⅔ of final remuneration.
In 1997/98, final remuneration is capped or limited to £84,000.
Therefore, the maximum allowable pension is ⅔ × £84,000 =
£56,000.

You may be forced to retire early, for example through ill-health.
Some schemes provide early retirement (ill-health) reduced
pension benefits, as well as death benefits (of up to 4 times final
salary) if death occurs before retirement (plus a return of personal
contributions). A spouse or dependant pension can also be given
of up to ⅔ of the maximum pension which the deceased would
have received at normal retirement date. Some schemes also
allow for this in death *after* retirement, for spouses or dependants.

The important factor (apart from the amount of your salary) is
related to the number of years' service which you have with that
particular employer. The more years' service you have, the greater
will be your tax-free lump sum and eventual pension from your
employer. As an employee, if you have fewer years' service, you
cannot simply put your own money directly into the pension
scheme and hope that you will have a higher pension accruing to
you, unless in a public sector scheme using additional voluntary

contributions (AVCs) to boost your pension. These types of schemes do not work in this way. The only way in which you can obtain a higher pension from your final salary scheme is by having more years' service allocated to you. With some schemes, it is possible to buy additional years' service, and if you do not have sufficient years' funding this may well be a strategy for you if it is not too expensive.

STRATEGY 19
Ascertain if you can purchase additional years' service and at what cost

---

Whilst an actuarial calculation is usually required to give you the exact figure, the following formula will give you a simplistic calculation of what you can expect as an employee in a final salary scheme. The formula is as follows:

$$\text{Pension} = \frac{N}{P} \times FS$$

STRATEGY 20
Contribute up to 15% into additional pension funding, through an AVC or FSAVC

An AVC will be offered by the pension provider to the final salary scheme, and will be administered *by the employer*. A free standing AVC (FSAVC) is one which you can choose yourself from many hundreds of different product providers and over which *you have control*. Whilst you cannot take a lump sum benefit from your AVC/FSAVC, unless you set it up under pre-1987 rules, it does increase the amount of the funds available which provide you with a pension, which could, in turn, increase the amount of the lump sum received from your employer in retirement.

Contributions to an AVC or FSAVC are tax deductible to the employee up to 15% of his or her remuneration. The 15% includes contributions required by the scheme, and for contracted-out money purchase schemes, employee rebates. Remuneration does not only include your salary, but also includes the value of your benefits in kind, such as the value of a company car.

Example:
As Tim does not have a company car, he would be entitled to make a contribution of 15% × £15,000 (his present salary) as an additional voluntary contribution each year. Tim could therefore contribute £2,250 as additional voluntary contributions, and have that amount as a deduction from his taxable income. This means that the Inland Revenue will essentially be funding 23% of Tim's contribution. If Tim had been a higher-rated taxpayer, the Inland Revenue would have been funding 40% of the contribution made as a result of its tax deductibility.

The salary cap of £84,000 (1997/98) applies to AVC/FSAVC schemes, so that the maximum contribution in 1997/98 will be 15% × £84,000, which is £12,600 p.a. or £1,050 per month.

If contributions to an FSAVC scheme exceed £2,400 p.a., a 'head room' calculation must be done to ensure that strict Revenue limits are not exceeded. Contributions are paid *net* of basic rate tax. Higher-rate taxpayers have their PAYE tax codes adjusted or claim through their tax returns.

Tim's gross contribution of £2,250 would build a fund of £240,000 in 25 years' time, assuming a rate of growth of 10%, at a net cost to him of £1,732.50 p.a. after tax. This would be inclusive of his contribution to the main final salary pension scheme fund. Some final salary pension schemes are what is known as 'non-contributory'. This means that the company he works for funds the entire pension scheme on Tim's behalf and the obligation is on the company to ensure that it has sufficient funds to be able to pay out this defined benefit.

STRATEGY 21
Establish what your maximum tax-free cash lump sum is if you are an employee of a company with an occupational pension scheme

---

In addition to the pension which Tim could hope to receive from the company final salary scheme, as well as an additional pension from his additional voluntary contribution scheme, he could also expect to receive as a commutation of pension, if elected, a tax-free lump sum benefit from his employer's scheme, which is usually calculated as a factor multiplied by the amount of annual pension receivable by him. For example, assuming that Tim has 15 years service, depending when he entered the scheme, the tax-free cash sum is determined as follows:

i) Pre-1987 schemes $15 \times \frac{3}{80} \times £20,000$ = £11,250 tax-free cash
ii) Post-1987 schemes $2.25 \times £5,000$ = £11,250 tax-free cash

Different rules relating to the amount of benefit apply, depending upon when Tim entered into the final salary scheme, both as a pension and as a tax-free lump sum which may be received. For example, under post-1987 final salary schemes, the maximum lump sum which Tim could receive is $2.25 \times$ his annual pension before commutation. The maximum cash lump sum representing two-thirds of the earnings 'cap' is $2.25 \times £56,000 = £126,000$.

Tax-free lump sums are determined from the following formulae:

i) Pre-1987 schemes – $1.5 \times$ final remuneration after 20 years' service (with many caveats).
ii) Post-1987 schemes – $2.25 \times$ initial annual rate of pension before commutation (includes the value of AVCs and FSAVCs) or $\frac{3}{80} \times$ final salary for each year of service up to a maximum of 40 years' service, whichever is greater. Therefore, one cannot have more than one and a half times final salary as a lump sum.

Final remuneration is determined according to various formulae and by the rules of the fund and may include the value of employee benefits.

i) Pre-1987 schemes – no cash limit.
ii) Post-1987 schemes – limited to the earnings cap which is £84,000 (1997/98).

Tim could also receive the benefits of a FURBS – a funded unapproved retirement benefit scheme – should his employer wish to contribute to this arrangement for him.

STRATEGY 22
If at maximum contribution levels, consider a funded unapproved benefit scheme

---

Unless Tim has income from another job, where there is no pension scheme, there is not much more that he can do for himself using existing tax legislation in respect of pension funding.

An employer may be in a position to give a super-charge boost to retirement funding (these aspects are covered in Chapter 8) but these types of schemes are only suitable for earnings over the earnings cap – £84,000 in 1997/98. If you are earning at higher levels, these may be suitable for you.

STRATEGY 23
Consider a salary sacrifice to boost your AVC fund contributions

---

This could be a sacrifice of salary (safely up to £5,000 p.a.), of a bonus, of a salary increase, or a benefit in kind.

Employer contributions would save on employer NI, and the employee could also pay less NI if earning between the lower and higher earnings band limits – however, watch out for reduced SERPS benefits.

The main disadvantages could be the effect on 'final remuneration' or 'pensionable salary' used to calculate other pension benefits and proper planning needs to be undertaken first. This sacrifice should only be contemplated by senior employees, and then not within ten years of retirement. Also, a reduction in salary may affect redundancy terms or mortgage income multipliers for instance. However, if funding is presently poor, and you are nowhere near maximum funding (or if your salary is over the pensions cap, then it may be an alternative to a FURBS), then consider this option.

Example:
Lesley earns £35,000 a year and wants to make the maximum permitted contribution to a scheme. However, her employer cannot contribute. Lesley could fund at a rate of

15% × £35,000 = £5,250, but to satisfy Revenue rules, there must be a 'significant' employer contribution. Lesley sacrifices £5,000, reducing her earnings to £30,000. She can now make a reduced AVC/FSAVC contribution of 15% × £30,000 = £4,500.

The total contribution will now be £5,000 (the sacrifice) *plus* the £4,500, making a total of **£9,500**.

The sacrifice has effectively *increased* the total employer and employee contribution from £5,250 to £9,500 and reduced take-home pay by only £3,272, despite the sacrifice of £5,000.

	Before sacrifice £	After sacrifice £
Salary	35,000	30,000
AVC	(5,250)	(4,500)
Personal allowance	(4,045)	(4,045)
Taxable earnings	25,705	21,455
Tax payable 20%	820	820
23%	4,969	3,991
Total tax payable	5,789	4,811
Take-home pay	23,961	20,689
Difference	–	(3,272)
Value of AVC	5,2350	9,500
Employer NI savings	–	500

Including the employer NI savings of £500 enables £10,000 to be invested, nearly *double* the previous amount!

If you are an employee in a money purchase occupational pension scheme

A money purchase group scheme or occupational scheme is one operated and administered by the employer for the benefit of the employees. Contributions may be made by both the employer and the employee to the scheme in much the same way as for a final salary scheme.

A money purchase group pension scheme differs from a final salary scheme in that, whereas a final salary scheme will purchase a pension as an exact proportion of final salary, where the costs of funding are difficult to establish each year as they are actuarially determined, a money purchase group pension scheme has *defined contributions*, but an undefined estimated end benefit. The employee is entitled to that amount of the scheme which has been allocated to him, which may not fully equate to a percentage of his final salary, as with the final salary scheme.

The occupational group money purchase scheme allows a tax-free lump sum as well as a pension, with amounts similar to a final salary scheme.

STRATEGY 24
If an employee of a money purchase occupational pension scheme, follow the strategies as for a final salary scheme

---

These strategies include:

- 15% of pensionable earnings as a contribution to an FSAVC or AVC (less contributions required by the scheme and, for companies, employee rebates).
- Find out what projected pension and maximum tax-free cash lump sums will be available at retirement.

In addition, establish whether your employer money purchase pension scheme has an AVC facility so that you can make additional employee contributions to ensure a fund large enough for your maximum retirement purposes (some funds have changed from final salary schemes to money purchase schemes to save on costs and this may mean lower pension benefits for you).

- Will the employer consider a FURBS to augment or increase your retirement funds if your earnings are over the earnings cap?

If you are an employee in a Group Personal Pension Plan (GPPP)

A group personal pension scheme (GPPP) is a collection of individual contracts between the employees and the pensions provider, which are linked by their employer's involvement. An employer may collect contributions centrally, pay the contributions, or part-pay them with the employees also contributing.

Over the last few years, these GPPPs have become more and more popular because employers can control costs and the scheme is easier to administer (in the same way that a money purchase scheme is). GPPPs may continue to represent an attractive alternative to occupational schemes for employers as:

- They avoid Pensions Act 1995 (PA 95) provisions.
- They are not subject to minimum funding nor the compensation scheme (PA 95).
- There is no limited price indexation (LPI) on contributions in excess of the rebates (PA 95).
- They aid cost control.
- Only involvement need be the remitting of contributions.
- One provider is preferable. However, employees may already be contributing to other plans and the employer could be involved in additional administration.
- Some schemes include automatic fund selection.
- Employer contributions can be made, but this is not compulsory as with occupational schemes. However, it is seen to be essential to provide adequate benefits at retirement.
- They may have the income withdrawal option. Always ensure that you have premium waiver with your plan. If you become disabled or cannot work through ill health, your contributions are paid for you.
- Higher age-related rebates are possible.
- Members have an arrangement outside employer control, but can benefit from economies of scale.
- Members may have some investment choice (this may be good or bad depending upon the acumen of the employee taking investment decisions).
- GPPPs offer full portability.
- The member can *continue* with contributions after leaving. However, it is seldom in the employee's interests to transfer from one money purchase scheme to another.
- There is flexibility to withdraw benefits from age 50 – members of a GPPP do not have to retire to do so, whereas occupational scheme members do.
- There are no limits on pensions benefits, unlike occupational pension schemes. Occupational schemes are subject to 15% of earnings from the employee, and 100% from the employer; GPPPs start at 17.5% and go up to 40% from the employee, depending on age.

Whatever the position you would *like* to be in (whether as a member of an occupational pension scheme or a group personal pension scheme), each type has advantages and disadvantages, depending upon whether you represent the employer or employee point of view.

STRATEGY 25
If considering the merits of which type of scheme to have, you require expert advice – get it

---

If you are a business owner or you are influential in choosing the type of scheme required, get expert advice for the best route and type, depending on your circumstances and those of the business.

Obtain comparisons and conduct regular reviews to make sure that you keep on track.

STRATEGY 26
If in a group personal pension arrangement, arrange to maximum fund your contributions

---

You and your employer may contribute between 17.5% and 40% of 'net relevant' earnings, depending on your age.

Contributions are also subject to the pensions cap (in 1997/98 this is £84,000).

See the table in the personal pensions section (Strategies 34 and 35) for more information.

STRATEGY 27
Consider a salary sacrifice to provide funding where your employer cannot do so

---

Salary sacrifice, as used for occupational pension schemes, can also be used as a valuable tool to fund a personal pension plan.

The most common method is to sacrifice a salary increase or a bonus entitlement, or a portion of salary itself.

Basically, the employee is sacrificing salary in return for an employer contribution. This could be most tax-efficient as you could save tax, if a higher earner, by investing your salary increase or bonus into a pension plan.

The employer will save 10% on National Insurance contributions on the amount sacrificed, as will the employee if earnings are between the lower and upper earnings limits. Watch out, though – lower National Insurance contributions could mean reduced SERPS benefits.

A particular benefit is if the employee is earning more than the earnings cap of £84,000 (in 1997/98), then a salary sacrifice could substitute for a FURBS, but only where the maximum funding level has not been reached.

The employer could agree to a group personal pension plan funded purely by salary sacrifice and the employer's savings on NI contributions arising from the salary sacrifice. Whilst this route may well increase pension benefits, it could also be seen to be inappropriate in some instances and proper caution is always advised.

Assuming a 5% salary sacrifice, the position is as follows (1997/98):

Employee salary	£10,000	£15,000	£30,000
5% sacrificed	£500	£750	£1,500
Employer's NI contribution rate	7%	10%	10%
NI saving	£35	£75	£150
Contribution to personal pension	£535	£825	£1,650
Effective contribution rate	5.35%	5.5%	5.5%

There are advantages and disadvantages with using this approach.

Advantages
- Better group rates are possible through savings on costs.
- The NI saving would not normally be made to the plan.
- Increased pension funding.
- No cost to the employer.

Disadvantages
- Reduces 'net relevant earnings' for pension contribution purposes.
- Reduces SERPS benefits if earning between the lower and upper earnings limits. However, note SERPS benefits are

calculated on average lifetime earnings and the reduction may be insignificant.

Larger salary sacrifices (over £5,000) may require Inland Revenue approval.

Employee not on any pension arrangement

If you are an employee where there is no occupational pension scheme and no group personal pension scheme, then you may form your own personal pension plan (PPP).

STRATEGY 28
If an employee with no personal pension plan, form your own

If you are not a member of an occupational pension scheme, or if you are a member, but only for death in service benefits, then you may make contributions to a personal pension plan, so long as you have 'net relevant earnings'.

Start your personal pension plan as soon as you can, maximum funding it if possible.

See the table in the personal pensions sections (page 43) for more information.

You may wish to choose an 'insured scheme' from a product provider, or perhaps one where you have greater investment flexibility, such as a self-invested personal pension plan (SIPP). Winterthur Life, for example, has one of the lowest charging structures – it only costs £500 to set one up (1997).

STRATEGY 29
Contribute even more into your plan by utilising past years' reliefs through carry back/carry forward provisions

---

Any contributions to a personal pension plan can be augmented and boosted by using *unused* tax reliefs applicable over the last six years. If you don't use them, you lose them, as the years go by.

You can make significant single premium contributions into your plan. We recently arranged one for a client where an *enhanced* allocation amount applied – his £10,000 initial investment had an extra 16% added to it – £1,600 – which was a tremendous booster for his plan.

If you have not utilised your maximum contributions each year, you may *carry forward* unused reliefs for up to six years. This enables you to make additional pension contributions *now* for those past years. The earliest year to commence the process in 1997/98 is 1991/92, unless you deem this year's contribution to have been paid last year, in which case you can go back to 1990/91.

'Carry back' enables members to have part or all of a contribution counted as being paid in the *previous* tax year, provided there is unused relief for that year. If there are no 'net relevant earnings' in the previous year, you may go back another year.

Employer contributions may not be carried back.

By using previously unused reliefs contributions to pensions can be greatly increased. This assists those who have not had the money in the past by enabling them to contribute when they do have it.

Example:
Indigo Brown has recently started his personal pension plan. He is age 46 and was born in 1951, on 2 April.

Age	Year of assessment	Net relevant earnings	Percentage relief	Maximum relief available
46	1997/98	£84,000	25%	£21,000
45	1996/97	£71,600	20%	£14,320
44	1995/96	£52,011	20%	£10,402
43	1994/95	£31,454	20%	£6,290
42	1993/94	£24,363	20%	£4,873
41	1992/93	£9,012	20%	£1,802
40	1991/92	£2,937	20%	£587
	Total			**£59,274**

Assumption: this is the 1997/98 tax year.

He must make his contribution for the current year and can then go back to the 1991/92 tax year. He would have to pay £21,000 into his plan by 1 July 1997. He then goes back to 1991/92 and begins to use up reliefs from that date onwards. The relief available for that year was £587. Once 1991/92's reliefs have been used, then go to 1992/93 and use up £1,802 worth of reliefs. In total, Indigo has £59,274 worth of reliefs to use up. Each contribution *reduces* the taxable income and therefore tax paid at the highest rates of tax – so use the Inland Revenue to fund your pension plan.

Greater reliefs are possible using a personal pension plan, if you are an older person, as 40% is the relief allowed from age 61 and over, whereas 20% is the largest allowable relief for old-style retirement annuities.

IF YOU ARE A DIRECTOR

You are most likely to be in one of the following positions:
- Director with no pension plan.
- Director who controls less than 20% of the business.
- Controlling director, usually with a smaller employer, or family-owned business.

If you are a director with no pension plan

You must be in a new business, or an awfully poor one! You have a wide range of options available to you, ranging through a personal pension plan (PPP), an executive pension plan (EPP), or a small self-administered scheme (SSAS). You may even persuade your employer to opt for an occupational final salary scheme on the same basis as one arranged for an employee.

STRATEGY 30
Directors can get even bigger reliefs for pension contributions (so can employed spouses)

Directors can make contributions two to four times greater than the self-employed by contributing to an executive pension plan (EPP), or a Small Self-Administered Scheme (SSAS). Both of these are occupational schemes subject to strict Inland Revenue rules.

TABLE SHOWING DIFFERENT CONTRIBUTION LEVELS FOR DIFFERENT
TYPES OF PENSION PLANS

Normal retirement age of 65

Plan	Age	Male	Female
EPP	40	34.39%	34.22%
EPP	50	48.03%	47.79%
EPP	60	55.18%	54.90%
SSAS	40	72.33%	87.36%
SSAS	50	67.85%	81.95%
SSAS	60	43.88%	53.00%
Self-employed PPP	40	20%	20%
Self-employed PPP	50	25%	25%
Self-employed PPP	60	35%	35%

Directors who control less than 20% of the company

These may belong to occupational schemes in exactly the same
way as employees, and are usually employees in any event. The
director may contribute up to 15% into an AVC/FSAVC, be given
FURB benefits and be eligible for a salary sacrifice to enable
pension contributions to be made where the employer is unable to
do so.

Directors controlling 20% or more of a company

Controlling directors are deemed to be in a position where their
influence in respect of pension contributions is so great that the
PSO (Pensions Schemes Office) has restricted certain of their
activities. For example, the calculation of 'final salary' will be 'the
highest average of the total emoluments from the employer over
any period of three consecutive years ending within ten years
before retirement, leaving service, or death' as opposed to the
other more generous definition, 'best of the last five years'.

In addition, controlling directors *cannot* be members of an
FSAVC scheme.

However, a controlling director can be a member of an

unapproved occupational pension scheme, which will provide assistance to those with earnings in excess of the earnings cap (£84,000 in 1997/98) – for example, a FURBS.

STRATEGY 31
All directors, executives and qualifying employees should maximum fund their schemes

---

Small or family company pension schemes are more likely to be executive pension plans (EPPs) or small self-administered pension schemes (SSASs).

Both must be approved by the Inland Revenue, with the member being entitled to a pension and a tax-free lump sum at retirement age:

Executive pension plans (EPPs) have an accelerated funding programme depending mainly on the member's age and years left to retirement. They are offered by life offices and pension providers, who usually manage the investments. Retirement dates range between age 50 and 75.

Small self-administered schemes (SSASs) are for company controlling directors or partners and selected employees, but must have less than 12 members and have the same retirement range of 50-75, as do EPPs.

Special rules apply to prevent directors from abusing SSASs in respect of contribution levels, investments undertaken and other areas.

The SSAS must not be invested solely in insurance policies and there are also borrowing restrictions on its funds, as well as on loans to the employer (up to 50% of assets after two years but until then only 25% a year).

From an investment point of view, the SSAS can hold commercial property, shares in a private company and shares in its sponsoring company (5% of assets).

Pension benefits which are payable are calculated as for other employer-owned occupational pension schemes.

STRATEGY 32
If not in a director-only, or executive, scheme,
consider setting one up

Generous contribution limits allow for funding of up to 200% of salary or more, depending upon your circumstances. Pension contributions are an ideal tax-efficient way to get profits out of the business into your hands – possibly better even than taking dividends or a bonus (see Chapter 8).

IF YOU ARE SELF-EMPLOYED

The self-employed may contribute to existing retirement annuity contracts or to personal pension plans (PPPs). The latter have been available since July 1988, when the last of the Section 226 retirement annuity contracts were sold.

As some readers may have existing retirement annuities to which they are contributing, they can continue to make tax deductible contributions in the hope of a higher tax-free lump sum.

STRATEGY 33
Continue with section 226 retirement annuity
contributions if it is only in your best interests
to do so

If not, change to a personal pension plan. Tax-free lump sums from retirement annuities have, generally speaking, higher tax-free levels (30-35%) than a personal pension plan (25%).

However, this is only the case if you will not be using the open market option in retirement. As soon as you do so, your tax-free lump sum reduces to that of the PPP – that is, 25%.

You may wish to switch to a PPP (personal pension plan) because of the more generous funding levels as you get older.

STRATEGY 34
Contribute for maximum funding levels whether PPP or section 226 retirement annuity contracts

---

The following are the maximum contribution levels as a percentage of earnings.

Age on first day of the tax year	Personal pension %	Retirement annuity %
35 or less	17.5	17.5
36-45	20	17.5
46-50	25	17.5
51-55	30	20
56-60	35	22.5
61 or more	40	27.5

From age 36, the build-up into personal pensions will be at a greater rate than into retirement annuities. The levels of contribution almost double for later ages.

If you intend to select the best annuity rates at retirement and can contribute *more* than the maximum amount into an old style retirement annuity, then consider changing to a personal pension plan.

New retirement annuities (Section 226 contracts) have not been available since 1988.

STRATEGY 35
Keep within the allowable funding limits or face tax penalties

---

You may inadvertently over-fund your personal pension plan by paying in too much, believing your contributions to be within the limits.

At the very least, these excess payments will be returned to you with or without interest. The Inland Revenue could tax you and apply penalties, especially if you had tax relief in the first place.

You cannot contribute an amount greater than the percentage of the pensions 'cap' on earnings. In 1997/98 this is £84,000 and applies to personal pension plans as it does to occupational schemes.

MAXIMUM CONTRIBUTIONS TO PERSONAL PENSION PLANS

Age at 6 April 1997	Personal pension contribution rate	Maximum amount
35 or under	17.5%	£14,700
36-45	20%	£16,800
46-50	25%	£21,000
51-55	30%	£25,200
56-60	35%	£29,400
61 and over	40%	£33,600

STRATEGY 36
Set up a PPP or an EPP for your spouse or partner

Spouses, or partners – in particular, women – are known not to have provided well for themselves, mainly because of non-income producing family or other commitments. Yet the spouse is often helpful and essential to a business and could even be paid in pension contributions (see Chapter 8).

STRATEGY 37
If you like more flexible investment options, choose a SIPP

A SIPP is a self-invested personal pension plan, set up at minimum cost, where you can direct your own investment activity on your contributions. You have very wide investment options, choosing from other pension fund investments, to investments in fixed property. The SIPP is ideal for partnership property purchase. It can be tailored to suit all circumstances. It is also the most appropriate for the transfer of other pension funds for the purpose of drawing down income from your fund during a deferred retirement period, especially when annuity rates are low. The one major advantage is that you need not be locked into the investment management of one life office alone. A SIPP's funds can be spread over a number of investment houses, thus ensuring maximum flexibility. It is this flexibility which gives a unique range of options, including staggering your retirement dates, phased retirement or income drawdown.

STRATEGY 38
Get additional tax reliefs and increase pension funding through carry back and carry forward provisions, using personal pension plans

---

See Strategy 29 for the full details. If you are self-employed or employed (but not a member of your employer's pension scheme) or you have more than one source of income which qualifies as 'net relevant earnings', then any unused tax relief can be applied from previous years.

By using previously available but unused reliefs, contributions to pension funds can be greatly increased. This assists those who have not had the money in the past to be able to contribute when they do have it.

STRATEGY 39
Get the Inland Revenue to fund as much of your pension plan as possible

---

This applies not only to personal pension contributions, but to all qualifying contributions to an approved pension scheme.

For PPPs, contributions can only be made from taxable earned income or 'net relevant earnings'. These *exclude* income from dividends or interest on investments.

Net relevant earnings are 'capped' at £84,000 in the 1997/98 tax year, on which contributions are based.

Contributions attract tax relief at higher rates of tax.

Example:
Consider the case of William McGee, age 52, who earns £41,000 taxable income per annum (1997/98).

	With contribution	No contribution
Gross taxable earnings	£41,000	£41,000
less pension contributions	(£12,300)	-
(30% × £41,000)		
less personal allowance	(£4,045)	(£4,045)
Taxable earnings	**£24,655**	**£36,955**
Tax payable 20%	£820	£820
23%	£4,727	£5,060
40%	-	£4,342
Total tax	**£5,547**	**£10,222**

The pension contribution made by William of £12,300 has reduced his tax payable by £4,675, which is his tax saving, the net cost of the pension contribution being £7,625 or 62%.

Because the pension fund itself grows tax-free and contributions are tax deductible, the Inland Revenue funds anything from 20% to 40% plus of your fund under current legislation. The tax-free aspect of your lump sum at retirement means that the Revenue has given you *at least* another 15% worth of investment fund towards your retirement. This is a total of *over* 55% worth of Inland Revenue incentives – not counting the fact that your pension fund grows tax free and may have received contracted-out rebates from the DSS and other freebies.

You must not fail to maximise your funding advantage whilst you have it – there is no better investment available today.

STRATEGY 40
Use profit-related pay to give employees the cash to make booster contributions

---

Whilst the government is resolved to phase out PRP – profit-related pay – the concept will still be with us for a couple of years and may still be used.

Under PRP, the employee can receive part of pay tax-free. The formula is 20% of pay, or £4,000 of the actual PRP received in the year, whichever is the lesser.

By combining PRP with additional pension contributions, one can achieve a gearing effect on the same money.

Example:
Lex Wright, age 39, earns £35,000 taxable income per annum.

	Before	**After**
Taxable earnings	£35,000	£35,000
less PRP	-	(£4,000)
less personal allowances	(£4,045)	(£4,045)
less pension contributions at 20% for PPP*	–	(£7,000)
Taxable income	**£30,955**	**£19,955**
Tax payable: 1997/98	**£7,822**	**£4,466**

* Use 15% for FSAVC/AVC

The net cost of the pension contribution is £3,644 (a total tax saving of £3,356) or 52%. By combining PRP with maximum pension relief, the Inland Revenue can annually pay about half of your pension contribution costs – at no additional cost to the business.

IF YOU ARE A PARTNER

The position of a partner is midway between the self-employed situation (where funding is via personal pension plans) and a company situation where one may find an occupational pension scheme, such as an SSAS. 'Partner' in this sense is defined as an equity partner in a business.

Where the partners group themselves together, and there are less than 12 of them, they could contribute to a small self-administered scheme (SSAS) (see Strategy 31). Where there is a larger group, a group personal pension plan is more usual (see page 32). Smaller partnerships may have individual personal pension plans, similar to the self-employed (see Strategies 33 to 40).

For a full understanding of how partners can not only retain wealth, but build it up, see Chapter 23 of *Wealth Strategies for*

Your Business by Tony Granger for a general overview and strategies where there is a complex structure.

STRATEGY 41
Increase pension funding to further reduce taxation and build wealth

---

Partnerships in England and Wales are not legal persona as they are in Scotland. In England and Wales, it is the individual members of a partnership who are trading and not the partnership itself.

However, for taxation purposes, income tax for the partners throughout the UK is assessed in the name of the partnership. Under self-assessment in 1997/98, and new partnerships from 6 April 1994, joint assessment is abolished. Partners are now directly assessed.

Once partnership expenditures and allowances are deducted from trading income, then the whole of business profits are treated as the partners' income and taxed under Schedule D.

After personal drawings, the balance of after-tax profits is usually loaned back to the business by the partner. This is represented by the *capital account* and is largely used to fund working capital and capital expenditure.

This capital account usually represents the *value* of the partnership share. Usually, by agreement, it is paid out in instalments on retirement or death, so as not to reduce working capital significantly at that time. This can create hardship for the retiree, especially if pension funding has been insufficient.

In connection with the above, some partnerships have a policy of maximising pension contributions. The retiring partner leaves his capital account behind, substituting the tax-free cash lump sum from his personal pension plan or SSAS arrangement for it.

As partnership profits are generated by the whole firm, of which the partner is a member, it is akin to the profits of a company in some ways. Value is reflected in compound growth pension funding instead of shares.

It is essential that partners get to grips with their retirement funding arrangements as quickly as possible.

STRATEGY 42
**Make sure you understand your partnership agreement
– don't leave behind more than you have to**

Study your partnership agreement carefully. I recently had a case where the partners in a business were responsible for their own maximum funding of pensions as their capital accounts were to be left behind in the business – financial disaster for my new client. He hadn't studied the 'form' and only woke up when his retirement date dawned and his pension fund was hopelessly under-funded.

Get things changed – there are ways to substitute capital account working capital for other finance. Once you retire, you have *no* control over what happens to the management of your capital account.

STRATEGY 43
**Maximise pension contributions as the repayment of
capital accounts may be slow**

As mentioned above, if the circumstances (and previous history of the firm) are such that slow repayments of capital accounts occur, then each partner either changes the system or makes maximum provision himself for tax deductible pension funding.

Pension funding is the major method of building wealth outside the business and of taking out pre-tax profits in the form of pension contributions.

STRATEGY 44
**Pay unfunded pensions and cash lump sums to
retiring partners**

The partnership *itself* can pay a pension to retiring partners. This will be deductible to the other partners in their partnership proportions. To qualify as earned income for allowances, the pension must:

- be paid in accordance with the partnership agreement or supplementary agreement.
- not exceed 50% of the average profit of the retiring partner for the best three of the last seven years before retirement.
- allow a tax-free cash sum of 25% of the notional accumulated sum to be taken.
- be allowed to increase and, where necessary, be paid to a spouse or dependant.
- allow 5% of net relevant earnings to provide term life insurance cover.
- be paid direct or by the purchase of an annuity.

Such a 'fund' may be used for the benefit of a partnership. No loans are allowed if a fund is established, but the fund can purchase commercial property from the partnership and lease it back on commercial terms.

Partners may, therefore, provide for pensions in a tax-efficient manner without having to set aside capital, if things have been left too late, or merely as an agreed course of action.

The unfunded scheme has its limitations, especially where profits fluctuate, and pensions will probably be lower than if conventionally funded. It should *not* be relied upon as capital may not be available at the exact time it is required.

STRATEGY 45
It may pay you to form a partnership with your spouse, or to provide employment to spread the pension funding burden

---

More taxpayers usually mean less taxes to pay, especially if spreading the load amongst family or relatives.

Paying salaries to employed spouses, or taking a spouse on in the partnership (even as only a 'sleeping partner'), provides the ideal opportunity for more pension funding and greater retirement independence.

See Chapter 8 for further details.

NON-WORKERS, OR THOSE WITH UNEARNED INCOME

People in this category may not have income from employment, but may have investment income or dividends acquired on inheritance, been given assets, been provided with housekeeping money, or whatever.

Unfortunately, the pensions saving route is blocked because of the rule on earned income being the only source of pension contributions. Personally, I think the rule is outdated and the pensions scheme office is reviewing it – if you pay any tax on income such as interest from an investment, you should be able to contribute to pension funding. Even if your money came from a tax-free source, then you should be allowed to pension contribute with it – only don't expect tax relief. However, our present system doesn't allow this.

STRATEGY 46
Build up your own retirement fund by saving regularly into growth funds

---

In addition to the investment spectrums given in Chapter 7, you could also consider savings into PEPs (Personal Equity Plans) which grow tax-free, have no capital gains tax payable on sale and are flexible – you can always have access to cash. If you don't mind a bit of investment risk (you may lose your capital), then a venture capital trust (VCT) allows some of your contribution to be tax deductible as it grows tax-free and shares, when sold, are free of capital gains tax. Income from PEPs and VCTs are tax-free.

Many people prefer to invest directly into equities, such as the privatisation issues; others prefer the concept of 'pooling' through investing regular amounts into unit trusts, investment trusts, open ended investment company schemes (OEICS), and endowment policies. Some prefer growth with capital protection, and many new plans include exactly that. It is entirely possible to *protect* your capital and achieve growth in your investment. Those approaching retirement, or who have retired and wish to preserve their capital, will be particularly attracted to this route. Others may prefer building society, bank or national savings investments, but these are more income-driven than growth oriented.

In addition, *and this applies to everyone*, whether employed or self-employed or not earning – look at what the State has to offer you and try to improve on that.

STRATEGY 47
**Make maximum use of what the State can provide to
ensure better funding for a financially secure
retirement**

The basic State retirement pension from April 1997 is £62.45 a
week.

- Make sure that you qualify for the full State pension. If not, it
  may pay you to pay into it, to secure additional years' worth
  of payment.

The State also provides the State Earnings Related Pension
Scheme (SERPS). This provides additional benefits to the State
retirement pension. The government has been trying to wean
people off SERPS and is committed to winding it down.

- Check your entitlement to SERPS and whether you are
  currently contracted into SERPS, i.e. whether you remain in
  the scheme or whether you *contracted out* by accepting the
  National Insurance contributions each year towards
  appropriate pension plans (APPs). Contact your local DSS
  office and complete Form NP38 for an estimate of your
  retirement benefits.

- It may pay you at this stage to contract *back in* to SERPS to
  retain entitlement to the benefit. Actuaries have established
  certain ages for males and females when it is better to
  contract back in, rather than remain outside the system. It is
  felt that certainly older people (over 55 for men and 47 for
  women) may receive more from SERPS than by substituting
  SERPS for a personal pension plan. Note this is only for that
  SERPS related contracted-out part – don't neglect your
  overall pension funding.

STRATEGY 48
Check your entitlements – the more from the state,
the less you need do yourself

The basic State pension for those males attaining age 65 is presently £62.45 per week (£3,247.40 p.a.) with an increased amount for a married spouse to £99.80 a week (£5,189.60 p.a.).

The additional amount provided by SERPS may have changed depending on whether you contracted in or out of SERPS. The following will give you an overview of how best to assess your options.

The State Earnings Related Pension Scheme (SERPS)

In 1988 the government announced that benefits provided by SERPS were to be reduced.

At present, about 12.5% of men and 7.5% of women as a percentage of the total adult population group, numbering over 5 million people, are members of the State Earnings Related Pension Scheme. Those millions of people who have 'contracted out' of SERPS will not lose that portion of their SERPS benefit which has already accrued. Members are mainly in the 25-50 age group, earning £15,000 to £25,000 as household income.

Whilst in 1908 Lloyd George gave retired men an old age pension of five shillings a week (20% of the national average wage, which is still the same today), the average life expectancy in 1908 for a male was 49 years – today it is 73. The government has long realised that State provided pension benefits were low and that people were living longer and will continue to do so. In 1961, it introduced the *graduated pension* to supplement the basic pension. This scheme operated from April 1961 to April 1975 and related benefits and contributions to earnings. The scheme worked on units credit of £7.50 per unit for men and £9 per unit for women.

For those in receipt of the graduated pension or still to receive it, the maximum supplement payable per week is about £7.

In April 1978, the government introduced the State Earnings Related Pension Scheme (SERPS) as an additional State scheme. It was for employees only and based on the National Insurance contributions you and your employer pay on your earnings between the lower earnings level (LEL) – now £62 per week (£3,227 p.a.) – and the upper earnings level (UEL) – now £465 per week (£24,180 per year).

The amount of your earnings which lies between these two limits is known as your 'band earnings'.

There have been a number of significant changes over the years, as the government attempts to wind down the SERPS in favour of private provision.

Originally, SERPS was supposed to provide a pension of 25% of band earnings if you retired in 1998 or later. The government intended to increase actual earnings during your working lifetime in line with increases in national average earnings up to retirement. Then it would choose the *average* of the best 20 years.

Of this national average earnings figure 25% would then be paid as the Earnings Related Pension, or a lifetime pension of 25% of your average salary.

If you reach age 60 (females) or 65 (males) before 6 April 1999, your pension would be 1.25% or ⅟₈₀th of the total notional earnings for all the years contributing to SERPS since 1978.

If, for example, you retire *before 6 April 1999*, and over those 22 years (from 1978 to 1999) you earned £252,864 in band earnings (an average of about £11,500 a year), then 1.25% of this is £3,160.80 p.a. Under the original SERPS scheme, if you were to retire by 6 April 2002, then the best 20 years' average of earnings was taken, which would have meant a SERPS pension of £3,376.30, using similar figures as before.

At present, we have a further reduction in SERPS payable, with it being phased out in the future. The present rules state that if you reach State Retirement Age after 5 April 1999, then SERPS will be reduced. It is no longer the average of the best 20 years, but now the average of your *whole working lifetime*. It is also the average of *band* earnings, not actual earnings.

On the former basis, if the average band earnings over the last 20 years was £13,505, then the SERPS pension was £3,376. On the new basis, if average earnings over your working lifetime were £9,300, then the SERPS pension would be £1,860 if you retire from the year 2009/2010 or later (20% of £9,300). There is a percentage reduction sliding scale if you retire between 1998 and 2010 from 25% in 1999/2000 down to 20% in 2009/2010 or later.

Importantly, SERPS also offers a *widows' benefit* and, from the year 2000, the widow must be aged 45 or over and/or have dependent children to qualify for 50% of the SERPS benefit.

Obtain DSS leaflet NP 32A for further information.

Since 1988, the government has been trying to get employees to give up their SERPS benefits in favour of private pension funding which would be funded by a portion of the employee's and employer's National Insurance contribution. In other words, if you took out a personal pension plan or contracted out through your employer's occupational pension scheme, then you lost your entitlement to SERPS (except for already accrued benefits). The idea was to provide an equivalent amount through a contracted-out scheme. This equivalent amount was represented by a guaranteed minimum pension or GMP.

To produce benefits equal to SERPS, the cost would be more expensive for women as they tend to live longer and retire earlier and more expensive for older people generally, who have less time to build up a fund. The initial rebate to contract out from 1988 to 1993 was 5.8% of band earnings, meaning that it *may* pay men to contract out up to age 50 and women up to age 40. The uplifted incentive (the 'bribe') increased these ages for men to 55-57 and women to 45-47.

The present rebate incentive for 1997/98 for contracting out of SERPS into final salary schemes is 4.6%, made up of 3% from the employer and 1.6% from the employee National Insurance contributions. The rebate into personal pension plans is based on age and ranges from 3.6% for a twenty-year-old to 9% for those aged 46 and above. There is also tax relief of 0.48% on the employee contribution to the employer.

You should review your SERPS entitlement by completing DSS form NP 38. There is nothing to stop you from contracting back into SERPS if you feel this will benefit you. Inform the DSS if this is your wish. Older people are best advised to remain in SERPS as they possibly may not have enough time to build up an alternative fund. Whether to contract in or out or to return to SERPS is a matter of personal choice based on your circumstances.

For example, a woman aged 29 who remains in SERPS could expect to receive a pension of 12.2% of her final earnings. If she were to contract out until State Retirement Age, her personal pension plan might give her a pension of 13.9% of her final earnings. However, if she were to contract out through a personal pension plan and then contract back in after 14 years, her total pension might *increase* to 15.8% of her final earnings.

As SERPS is an issue which depends on personal circumstances, you need to ascertain which of the routes will give you the best deal in retirement – contracting out, staying in, or coming back in having been contracted out.

After taking into account what the State has to offer, the balance of your pension funding should be made yourself to ensure a comfortable and happily financially secure retirement.

State pension benefits should always be taken into account when assessing your retirement needs, and will on *average* account for about 15-20% of a retired couple's income requirements.

The final objectives with regards to financing your retirement will also determine whether you will merely make contributions into a pension scheme, or whether you will, in addition, have to build up a separate investment portfolio to provide you with later income in order to meet your requirements.

The choice of pension plan is, therefore, most important, particularly where you have the flexibility to be able to choose which arrangement suits you best.

STRATEGY 49
Compare charges, costs and performance for best results

Hardly a weekend goes by without financial commentators in the money pages of the national press having something to say about charges, costs and performance of personal pension schemes. Some pension plans have very high costs, but they can also deliver on performance and the net result to the individual could well be higher than a pension plan which has a low cost structure but inadequate performance.

If a company was to make no charges at all, then this does not mean to say it will be best on performance.

Please bear in mind that *different scenarios* arise for different ages and years to retirement and the amount of premiums payable. Some companies have higher charging structures in earlier years than average; others have lower charges.

It is therefore *not true* to say that because a company has very low charges, it will outperform a higher charging structured company – in fact, the reverse may be the case, if investment fund performance is brought into account. Track records on performance, charges and payouts could mean up to £200,000 *more* for the same premiums in fund values over 30 years, at least £50,000 more over 30 years and at least £10,000 more over 10 years where the monthly premium is £300 per month.

For example, some of the new direct line pension providers may offer a very low charging structure, but they have no track record as far as performance is concerned. Some of them do not offer waiver of premium on their contributions, which any financial adviser worth his salt should be offering to you in case you become disabled or cannot work, in which event the product provider provides the premium contributions on your behalf. Yet, on the other hand, it has been known for the charging structures of some product providers to be so high that they actually eat up more than 25% of what your fund value would have been. It therefore makes sense to ensure that you create the necessary balance between lower charging structures and higher performance capability from pensions providers. Alternatively, some product providers do have charges which are competitive at higher premium levels. The bottom line is to shop around and make comparisons.

The major thrust of consumer attack as far as pension providers have been concerned, has not only been to demand a lower charging structure for pension plans but also to demand the best performance possible. Many pension providers seeking to meet these consumer demands will be driven out of business, as the provision of pensions business will become unprofitable to them. This will lead to some pensions offices ceasing to underwrite any new business and merely becoming closed investment funds, whilst others will merge with larger life offices and pensions managers, or will demutualise in order to grow bigger through the injection of shareholders' funds. Thus, the strength of the life office or pension provider where you invest your money is also a criterion which needs to be taken into account when making your investment decisions with regard to pension plan funding.

Employers who operate pension schemes should also be taking these factors into account, in reviewing what they have, and in seeking to find out what the market has to offer them. In fact, the new Pensions Act of 1995, which came into effect in April 1997, is a piece of legislation which has enormous implications for those operating, sponsoring and administering pension schemes. My message to employers is to make sure that they regularly review their pension schemes, taking into account possible uplifts in investment performance, as well as the possibility of streamlining their pension schemes, so that they, and their employees, get a better deal.

STRATEGY 50
Invest in pensions for better tax-free growth

Taking into account all the factors discussed above, you will now be in a position to maximise your pension funding, both with a view to maximum contribution levels, as well as to the optimum type of plan which is most suitable for your circumstances and needs.

Whilst you may physically be in a position to make the contributions required in order to build up your retirement, it may not be legally possible for you to make that level of contribution. At this point consider, from your own previous best expert calculations, the amount of monthly contribution which you need to make in order to reach your target fund. You will have completed this exercise in Chapter 2. If, in your opinion, you can only legally make a certain level of pension contributions (obviously you must be able to afford these), the balance of what you would have put into pension scheme funding must now go into alternative investments.

Purely from an investment point of view, investments made into approved pension scheme funding are one of the best mediums for making investments. The contributions going into the fund are tax deductible to you and there is no tax on the growth in your pension plan. At retirement date (except for AVC/FSAVC), you can expect to enjoy a tax-free lump sum from your accumulated fund. Moreover, the pension, based on the balance of your fund, will be taxable. Pension funds, therefore, are very tax efficient, and investment efficient, vehicles.

STRATEGY 51
Develop your alternative investment strategy

Your best alternative choice would be a low costed Personal Equity Plan, where the investment growth is tax-free, and any income which you receive is also tax-free. Whilst contributions to your Personal Equity Plan (PEP) are not tax deductible to you, the plan does enjoy tax-free growth and you have access to it at any time. In fact, many people who are unable to contribute to pension plans use a PEP as an alternative to their pension scheme funding.

Latterly, if you enjoy a higher risk preference, you may wish to invest into a venture capital trust where the growth and income within the trust also accrue to you tax-free, and your contributions going into the venture capital trusts (VCTs) are presently tax deductible from your actual tax liability at up to 20% of the investment made, which qualifies. These, and other investment possibilities, are discussed in Chapter 7 which relates to your investment strategy before and after retirement.

Pension planning can play a most important part with regard to your overall tax planning and the making of pension contributions can significantly reduce your taxable income, possibly from one tax band to another. This, in turn, creates a greater level of net disposable income to yourself, which can again be applied to additional investment funding.

The vast majority of future retirees will mostly be left to their own devices in structuring a pension plan from their own net after-tax resources. However, in certain instances, the business or the employer may be able to assist in the creation of personal wealth at no additional cost to itself. One of these areas is whether it is better to take a dividend or a bonus from the business or whether greater levels of personal wealth can be built through a combination of these and making additional pension contributions. This aspect is covered in Chapter 8. Whichever your route towards super-charged retirement plan funding, you will, by now, have the understanding of the magnitude of the task in hand and what has to be done to achieve your objectives.

STRATEGY 52
You *can* build a £1 million pension fund!

It's no bad thing to set your sights high and then to aim for that target – you may have 40 years in which to do it, so why not? Let's see how positive-thinking people feel about the table below:

**Contribution amounts required at various ages
to have £1 million at age 65**

Age	Term years	Contribution p.a.	Interest 10% compound p. a.	Value
20	45	£1,265 (£105 p.m.)	10%	£1m
25	40	£2,055	10%	£1m
30	35	£3,355 (£280 pm.)	10%	£1m
35	30	£5,530	10%	£1m
40	25	£9,250 (£770 p.m.)	10%	£1m
45	20	£15,900	10%	£1m
50	15	£28,600 (£2,383 p.m.)	10%	£1m
55	10	£57,100	10%	£1m
60	5	£150,000	10%	£1m

*The above table assumes no charges and is shown at one rate of
interest (10%) as opposed to the more generally accepted range
of rates at 6%, 9% and 12%.*

If age 20, then save £105 per month; at 40, you save £770 per
month; at 50, save £2,383 each month to make your million – it
will take less if contributions are tax deductible or if fund growth
is higher than expected.

Key points summary

- This chapter deals with the various types of pension plans
  available, depending on employment circumstances and what
  the State has to offer.
- It deals with the levels of contributions which may legitimately
  be made into approved pension funds, both by an employer and
  an employee, and also takes into account the circumstances of
  the self-employed and partners.
- Charging structures, investment performance and the strength
  of the product provider are serious factors which need to be
  taken into account in determining which plan to choose.

- Restrictive limitations on pension funding will require additional investment funding in order to meet your retirement objectives.
- Saving for a £1 million pension fund.

Action plan

I am _____ (director/employee/partner/self-employed)
I am a member of, or contributing to, the following pension schemes:
Occupational scheme (employee) ❏ Director's scheme or SSAS ❏
Personal pension plan/retirement annuity as director/employee, self-employed, partner ❏ Other ❏

I wish to do more pension funding

1. I can contribute £_____ per month to pension funding.
2. I am *allowed* to contribute ___% i.e. £_____ per month.
3. Investment term: years to retirement _____
4. Investor risk profile: cautious/balanced/speculative _____
5. View on charges – prefer:
    No commission, pay fees   ❏
    Self-invest personal pension   ❏
    Set-up charges and on-going charges   ❏
    Life office, usual charges   ❏
    Charges more important than performance   ❏
    Performance more important than charges   ❏
6. Check on additional years' service buyback and the cost (if an employee) ❏
7. Check to see if an AVC or FSAVC is possible alongside your employer's fund.
    AVC ❏   FSAVC ❏
    15% of salary £_____ p.m.
8. Check with employer about a FURBS contribution if at maximum funding ❏
9. Write down your preference for alternative investments here (such as PEPs, TESSAs, VCTs etc) _____
    _____
10. Do the same exercise for your spouse.

CHAPTER 4

Avoid the 10 Biggest Mistakes Made by Retirement Planners

> *A great deal of what we see depends on what we are looking for.*
> **Marty Allen**
> *Youth is a blunder; manhood a struggle; old age a regret.*
> **Disraeli (1804-1881)**

Objective: To pinpoint various areas of which to be aware in the retirement planning process. To highlight major areas of concern which may be omitted by your retirement planner, or which you need to know about to become your own financial expert

Retirement planning is both a science and an art form. It is a science in that we are dealing with an exact monetary contribution and calculation to produce a defined result at a pre-determined date. It is an art form when subjective desires associated with retirement planning need to be taken into account. Retirement planning is based on expected social and human need adjustments, which are usually associated with the lack of adequate money at that time – for example, moving to a smaller house, eating fewer meals, dealing with increased leisure time, and considering how best to entertain the grandchildren and provide for them. Our concern here, though, is more with retirement planning as a science because it could enable you to stay in the same house if required, still eat three meals a day, enjoy the leisure pursuits of your choice, and also have time for your grandchildren.

It is important to note the difference between retirement planning and pension planning. Retirement planning *encompasses* pension planning – but also includes investment planning, long-term care and health planning, tax and investment planning, and estate planning. Within this scenario, pension planning is only one aspect – retirement planning includes diverse options such as whether you will be able to pay off your mortgage at retirement, retain the company car as your own, invest wisely and so on.

Your retirement planner, therefore, should be given a very broadly-based view of what your need requirements before, as well as after, retirement are going to be. This would necessarily relate to you in your personal capacity, as well as to you in your business capacity – for example, as owner of a business wishing to sell it at the time of retirement. It is therefore important that all of your objectives are taken into account, not only those which deal with pension funding.

THE 10 BIGGEST MISTAKES OR OMISSIONS MADE BY RETIREMENT PLANNERS

1. Not taking all your circumstances into account

Ultimately you work to retire. Apart from protection and health insurance coverages, your investments, pensions, the sale of the business, are all planned towards one end – having enough cash or income at retirement in order to secure a happy future. Watch out for the isolationist retirement planner, who is only trying to sell you a pension plan. Make sure you get a written report, which outlines your financial planning objectives and recommendations, taking into account your risk profile with regard to investing, and a usable action plan. *Be extremely wary of 'single need' salesmen as you will, in all likelihood, have multiple needs which require satisfaction.*

2. Not having a clear focus on retirement funding – becoming easily distracted

The inclination of some retirement planners is to give you investments because they are more saleable, or because 'everyone should have one'. Again make sure that, after careful analysis, a TESSA, PEP, or even a pension plan is the *right retirement vehicle for you*. If you go to a PEP specialist for retirement planning, you can bet your boots that's exactly what you'll be investing in – a PEP, not a pension. Similarly, a building society adviser is going to be concentrating more on building society products, and likewise with one who advises on National Savings investments. *Ensure that you have a balanced portfolio of both growth and fixed interest investments.*

3. Funding for tax and not benefit reasons – you may never have enough at retirement if you follow this route

If you need to have 100% of your working salary as retirement income, then you will be funding for benefit reasons. Some of your retirement funding may come from pension funding and some will come from the income and capital growth generated by your investments. However, if you are merely funding for tax reasons, you may never achieve your objectives. For example, current pension fund legislation dictates how much you may put into a pension scheme which is tax relievable to you and, indeed, you may only use what are known as 'pensionable earnings', or 'net relevant earnings', to do so. At retirement, maximum pension funding will only allow you two-thirds of your final salary and the pensions funding cap will apply. Any surplus funding will be returned to you and you will pay tax on it. The whole of the UK pensions legislation is littered with restrictions on what you can and cannot do. *Make sure you fund for the benefits you require, by examining all possibilities, not only those with tax restrictions.*

You may also be tempted to make investments for tax reasons (for example, a portion of the investment is tax deductible to you or the income is tax-free) but, in accordance with your own risk profile, you should perhaps be in a different type of investment, rather than one which just gives tax breaks. *Make sure your retirement planner is aware of your concerns and that your portfolio objectives meet your circumstances and needs.*

4. Choosing the incorrect pension fund and pension provider – which could cost you up to 25% or more, in valuable fund benefits

It is important that your broker or planner assists you with making the right choices in respect of which pensions company to use, as well as which funds to go into. Indeed, this applies to all investments, including endowment policies, personal equity plans, unit trusts, investment trusts, venture capital trusts and others.

Most astute financial planners are very conscious of the high charging structures of some products and the poor performance of others on a consistent basis. This is possibly a good reason to seek independent financial advice, or merely to deal with a fee-based financial planner, thus minimising the effect of charges on your investments.

Having said that, a high charging product provider does not necessarily mean that investment performance will be poor, but a high charging product provider which also has poor investment performance means that your investment is on a hiding to nothing. It is up to you to ensure that you have a reasonable spread of investment and pension funds and that you monitor these on a regular basis. A flexible SIPP is one such plan which allows you to have a wide range of insurance company funds from different product providers within one pension.

If your retirement planner is doing his job properly, he should be spending many hours researching your personal situation and then coming up with the best plans for you. This is a critically important function and your retirement planner will need to be adequately rewarded for providing this service. However, high charges and commissions do deplete the growth potential of your investment plans as the compounding effect of growth will occur from a lower base. There has been a general move towards fee-based financial planning in respect of pensions and investments over the years and a realistic fee would be 0.5-1% per annum for servicing your investment if it is performing well.

5. Assuming that your employer is looking after you or, worse still, that you are looking after yourself

Complacency brought about by not having to do anything positive, believing that your financial planning needs have been fully taken care of, is one of the biggest traps into which you can fall. Some retirement planners are not fully conversant with your employee benefits and it is up to you to make sure they are appraised of all the details before they advise you. It may even be that your retirement planner, with your help, approaches your employer in order to make your employee benefits more tax efficient for you. Some businesses offer flexible employee benefits where there is a wider range of choices available, and you should be aware of these.

Where you are confident that you are making the best choices for yourself without any independent financial advice, and are merely instructing the retirement planner to undertake certain action, then you only have yourself to blame should things not work out as you expected. Many retirement planners are not forceful enough with their clients in insisting that a full review be done for them, if only as a second opinion.

Make sure that you are conversant with the benefits offered by your employer or, if you are a business owner or partner, that your broker or financial adviser keeps you fully informed as to what is available.

Remember that you and your employer may have conflicting points of view as to what will be adequate. An employer may wish to spend as little as possible on employee benefits, thus saving on costs, whilst you will wish the employer to spend *as much as possible* to assist you with your own wealth creation. You can be more proactive by assisting your employer to obtain the best value from your employee benefits. Many employee benefits are, in fact, wasted, as employees do not regard them as benefits. Remember, the more the business pays, the less you will have to pay out of your own back pocket in order to make up any shortfalls. It is thus most important that both the employee and the employer work together as much as possible within the employer's budget. I have known employees increase their benefits by up to 50% merely through funnelling what they would have paid for themselves from after-tax income, through their employer, in order to achieve greater savings through group-costed benefits.

Often what the retirement planner does not do is to advise you on your employee benefits where there may well be better options for you, such as buying back years of service into a final salary scheme, as opposed to making payments as additional voluntary contributions.

6. Not utilising maximum tax reliefs as provided under the legislation

In my 15 years practising as an independent financial adviser and retirement planner, I have actually come across very few instances where individuals have made maximum use of their contribution allowances. I am not referring to those who don't have the means to make higher level contributions. Rather, I am referring to those individuals who could have done more but didn't. For example, those with personal pension plans may contribute between 17.5% and 40% of their pensionable income depending on their age at the time. Employers in smaller companies may contribute up to and beyond 200% into executive pension plans for directors and even their spouses who are employed.

Where the self-employed or those entitled to personal pension plans are concerned, the carry back/carry forward provisions entitle them to mop up any unutilised pension fund relief going back six years. Yet, very few people know about this method of funding, let alone *use* it.

Always ensure that your retirement planner takes into account the full spectrum of reliefs available to you and at least brings them to your attention for consideration.

7. Receiving and not noticing incorrect calculations and projections which could leave you seriously underfunded

It is vital to check all figures and calculations, as well as future projections. This is particularly true in the case of transfer values from one pension scheme to another, the amount available from your fund at retirement, the amount payable from annuity providers, and figures involving tax calculations and future projection forecasting.

In a number of recent cases, one or two product providers have made serious miscalculations on the value of funds. In one such case, the value of a pension fund was under-calculated by well over a third by the life office concerned. The mistake was actually picked up by the client, not by the retirement planner in question. Whilst mistakes do happen, you don't want them to happen to *you*! Wrong forecasts, or projections based on incorrect assumptions, could have serious implications for your financial wealth when you get to retirement. *Err, rather, on the side of caution, using more conservative figures instead of more speculative ones.*

8. Not having a retirement countdown plan leading to big reductions in your tax-free cash

Not planning properly can cost you dearly. If you are planning to use the tax-free portion from your pension fund to pay off your mortgage at retirement and thus reduce your debt, to repay your school fees loan, to purchase a new motor vehicle, to make gifts to your children or a host of other requirements, ensure that you are adequately funded so that you can achieve these objectives whilst not leaving yourself short of retirement income.

If you had taken a longer-term view, you would have begun your debt reduction process a lot earlier, speeding up the capital repayment on your mortgage, or reducing your business loan before you retired. Naturally, there is a place in retirement and investment planning to take account of liabilities which need to be reduced from your tax-free lump sum on retirement. For many, this is the only way in which those debts will be reduced. For others who have not planned properly, it could mean using up the whole of your tax-free lump sum for aspects other than the production of more income in retirement.

It may well be sensible to increase your retirement funding in order to provide a larger tax-free lump sum in retirement. As your pension contributions are tax deductible, if you do use your tax-free lump-sum in this way, it would ultimately mean that the Inland Revenue had subsidised a part of your liability reduction programme. Some may see this as astute financial planning.

Financial planners who fail to advise you adequately in this area should have their attention drawn to your retirement countdown programme, which will reflect the various liabilities to be satisfied at various dates before and at retirement.

9. Using your directors' pension scheme as a bank or property storage facility – this could leave you with inflexible options on retirement

Make sure that your business objectives and your retirement planning objectives do not conflict. 'Director only' pension funds can provide loan facilities back to the company and may also be used to purchase commercial property. The objective of a pension fund is to make sure that there is sufficient *liquidity* within the fund to provide you with a pension in retirement. If assets held within the pension fund are incapable of realisation, you may not be able to retire adequately from it. Likewise, if the pension scheme has been used to fund loans to the company, and the company has been unable to repay these loans or has gone into liquidation, you could find that your fund is severely depleted.

The same applies to the self-employed who may have self-invested personal pension plans which are capable of holding fixed, yet possibly unrealisable, assets. Whilst it may be good business sense at the time, it could also prove to be financially disastrous for you in retirement. I have come across a case where all the members of a well-known rock group set up their own director-only pension schemes, which invested heavily into commercial properties. When the bottom fell out of the property market, their pension scheme assets were showing negative returns and were incapable of realisation. What they thought was a good investment in property, has turned out to be a nightmare for their advisers, as these schemes are totally illiquid and incapable of providing a pension.

Unless you have adequate alternative resources, make sure that your retirement planner informs you of the disadvantages, as well as the advantages, relating to your business investment decisions.

10. Not covering all the bases

You may not have explored all the funding options available to you. For example, if you are an employee, you should know about AVCs (Additional Voluntary Contributions allied to your main fund), as well as free-standing AVCs which can be purchased from any life office. Have you considered buying back service into a final salary scheme as opposed to making contributions to an AVC or an FSAVC? Have you considered going back into SERPS if you were previously contracted out? Have you been given advice on switching your unit-linked fund to a with-profits or a safety fund as your retirement date gets near? Are you taking advice on how to get your life cover tax deductible if you are entitled to a personal pension scheme, and how to protect your pension payments, should you become disabled and you cannot work?

In fact, how many retirement planners actually do *prepare you for retirement*? Were you on a retirement countdown programme before you read this book? How do you know that you are going to get the best advice as you approach the critical retirement date? Will you be placed into the worst or the best annuity options? Do you wish to preserve your pension fund for your dependants and heirs? Are you reconciled to possibly losing the unused value of your pension scheme in whole or in part, should you die too soon? If you have changed your job, or lost it, when should you transfer your funds, and when should you leave them where they are? What are the options, should you wish to take early retirement, or how late can you leave it before you actually retire?

Most of these questions can be well answered by the majority of good retirement and personal financial planners. Yet, there are a few who may never ask *any* of the above questions. As you become your own financial expert, you will very quickly ascertain whether the level of advice which you are receiving now, and that you can expect in the future, is satisfactory.

Some of the mistakes made by retirement planning advisers are not intentional – they are merely acts of omission. Yet, for the retiree, not having all the facts at your disposal, and not knowing the various options which may be taken, can severely damage your wealth as well as your peace of mind in retirement. *If in any doubt, take a second opinion.*

Key points summary

- The major retirement planning traps, mistakes and omissions are discussed, as well as the potential dangers inherent in receiving incorrect advice, or not enough of it.
- The multiplicity of options available throughout the funding process, and those that have to be taken at retirement and after it, all add up to the fact that anyone seriously wishing to maximise their retirement potential should engage an astute retirement planner.
- It is important that the retirement planner knows about your employee benefit structure, the pension arrangements within a business, your objectives, and is able to provide a full range of options for you to consider in line with your personal circumstances.

Action plan

1. Choose a retirement planner to review your position, if only to confirm your own opinion.
2. Prior to your meeting, draft a list of questions to which you need answers.

3 The person who sold you your pension may not necessarily be the right one to guide you through the maze of retirement decision-making which you will require. It's your financial future at stake – be prepared to switch horses if you can get a better track on which to run.

4. If you feel you have already made costly retirement planning mistakes, take immediate remedial action.

CHAPTER 5

Taking Critical Retirement Decisions

> *To everything there is a season and a time to every purpose under the heaven.*
> **Ecclesiastes 3:1**
> *People don't plan to fail; they just fail to plan.*

Objective: To make critical retirement planning decisions at various phases in the retirement planning process; to help overcome dilemmas associated with critical decision-making, which may affect your whole future

People approaching retirement need to formulate their retirement planning to best advantage by maximising pension funding and investments to provide income for their remaining years, having taken care to eliminate liabilities and mitigate the incidence of taxation. Decisions also need to be made such as how you are going to spend your retirement years, and if you are to continue work on a part-time basis.

The decision-making process is only as good as the accuracy of the information on which you base your decisions. You will make better decisions if you have full information, and a wide range of options to consider which are appropriate to your circumstances. Some decisions you can make alone, but others may require expert assistance and research and, even then, as time passes, you may wish to make changes as your personal circumstances themselves change. This is what adequate retirement planning is all about. It is a series of decision-making processes, not only based on the options available to you, but on whether you are capable of fulfilling the requirements underlining each option or, indeed, whether you want to.

This chapter will help you to build a critical retirement path all the way through the retirement process. Some periods are more critical than others. For example, decisions taken at the actual act of retiring may greatly increase or decrease your wealth potential and your prospects for a successful retirement as, once these decisions are made, they are often irreversible – such as the taking of an annuity, which type to take and which product provider to use.

Think of it this way. You've been given 10 weeks off work and have decided to use the time to go on a long vacation. Excited by the prospect, you sit down, surrounded by travel brochures, notebook and pen, and start to plan. Suddenly you realise just how much preparation is involved! First of all, you have to decide on your destination; next, you need to decide who will accompany you; then there's the cost, the clothes and other items you need to pack. You view your wardrobe with dismay! How will you get there? Will you need travel insurance and medical coverages? The dog needs to go into kennels, the household bills can't be left on the doormat for 10 weeks – it looks like time to call on the neighbours and co-opt some help.

Next, imagine that your holiday is not for 10 weeks – it's for 20 years, or more. What sort of preparation is needed *now*?

Retirement is an important enough event to take time out to plan effectively and make the necessary preparations – just as you would for a vacation.

The vast majority of people are inadequately prepared for a life in retirement. Whilst there are many books on the subject, they mainly deal with the social and economic aspects applicable to you once you are retired, but there has not been one which actually takes you through the process relating to the financial side of ensuring a happy retirement. Most have sections on how to build up funds, make pension contributions and ensure that investments are made but, again, none deal with the critical decision-making process without which your retirement could end up in disaster. You could have spent your lifetime building up adequate funds but taking the wrong decisions at retirement could then lock you into inflexible income streams and the possible loss of your capital on death, resulting in inadequate provision for your dependants.

For some, the prospect of retirement can be very stressful or alarming. For others (particularly those who are fully prepared for it), it is the culmination of a long lifetime's work, and something to which they can look forward, giving opportunities for new ventures. Perhaps you plan to travel, spend more time with children and grandchildren, or pursue leisure and cultural activities. However, those who have made a lot of money know how easy it is to lose it, and the most speculative investor pre-retirement suddenly has a total aversion to risk and becomes the most cautious investor imaginable. This is only natural.

Some of the biggest dilemmas facing people about to retire are that they won't have enough money to live on in the face of an uncertain economic future – for instance, inflation may get out of hand – or that they haven't saved enough in the first place, and therefore their spending options are restricted. Major life eventualities such as the possibility of going into long-term care can bring about an increase in costs far in excess of normal retirement provision. Over 20% of those aged 80 and over are in residential care homes or other long-term care programmes.

Let us now critically examine the various options available and the tasks which must be undertaken to ensure a happy and successful retirement.

Pre-retirement decision-making

STRATEGY 53
Decide on your long-term funding objectives

From previous chapters, you should, by now, have a full understanding of the task in hand in order to satisfy your retirement funding requirements. Not only will you have decided what your target retirement fund amount is, but you will also know exactly how much should be funded in order to meet this objective.

You will have seen the effect of the cost of delaying your funding programme by only one year. You will also have a rough idea of what amount should be funded on a monthly basis in order to support your retirement funding programme.

Even though you know it may well not be possible to be 100% successful with your funding programme, this need not necessarily deter you, as you will find out later in this book that there are ways of increasing your income in retirement as well as your capital.

For most people, the bulk of retirement funding is likely to occur only later on in life because of lack of net disposable income due to family commitments, or the effect of redundancies and general instability and insecurity in the workplace. A major stumbling block, however, may well be your own pre-conceived or misinformed ideas. People who have pension schemes provided by employers fully believe that those employers are going to look after them adequately by fully funding their pension schemes. When you undertake your own investigations, the chances are that you will see that this is patently not the case. Do not rely on your employer for maximum funding. In most cases you will find there is a shortfall in your eventual requirement and *you* will have to make up the difference.

Critical retirement decisions to be made at this stage are:

ACTION

- Decide on your normal retirement date.
- Decide on the total amount which needs to be funded for. £_____
- Decide on how you are going to provide this funding and how much can be funded monthly and annually. £_____
- If you require flexibility in retirement, take out adequate life insurance now – for at least the value, or a proportion, of the eventual total amount for which you are funded, or the size of fund you expect at normal retirement date. *Life cover required:* £_____
- If you have to fund school fees, or university and tertiary education fees, consider a school fee funding programme where the repayment vehicle for school fee loans is funded from your tax-free lump sum from pension funding. This can be most tax-efficient and is one of the few ways to build up a pension in retirement whilst having the Inland Revenue ultimately pay for a large proportion of your school fees through the tax deductibility of your pension contributions. Most people find it difficult to

pay school fees and fund for retirement. At least this way you pay school fees pre-tax and *also build up a pension fund.*

ACTION Investigate/ ignore

- Decide when your mortgage on your house or other property is due to be repaid. Although you may have a repayment vehicle in place, such as an endowment policy, excess cash may well be put to better use by speeding up your mortgage capital repayments to pay off your house up to 10 years earlier. Not only will you save thousands of pounds' worth of interest but your house will be paid off early and you would then have the endowment policy or other repayment vehicle to be used towards your retirement funding.

- Decide now what your proposed business exit options are going to be. Will you want to sell your shares? How will the partnership ensure that sufficient funding is available to pay you out? Does the partnership agreement have sufficient clauses to cover lifetime events such as death, disability or retirement? Can you sell your shares at retirement date? Is there a market for your shares? Would other shareholders be prepared to purchase your shares, or should you be looking to management or an employee share in a trust?

Investigate options/ ignore

- Decide *now* whether you will be partly responsible for looking after an elderly relative, parent or dependant in your retirement years. Decide whether you need to begin planning for this contingency now, and how it will affect your own funding requirements.

Investigate/ ignore

- Make a decision to examine critically your present outgoings and expenditures compared to your present income and see where savings can be made which can be diverted towards your investment and retirement planning.

Make a list of present income and expenditures

- Decide whether you wish to be your own financial expert, or whether you wish to appoint a financial adviser to assist you with your various planning activities.

Self/adviser

- Make a conscious decision as to the exact date that your retirement planning process is going to begin, using the countdown chart in Chapter 2.

ACTION

- Begin the estate planning process now, by ensuring that your wills are up-to-date.

See solicitor

- Make sure that you qualify for maximum State benefits in retirement by obtaining form number NP 38 from the DSS and requesting information now on your eligibility for the State pension, as well as for the additional State pension (SERPS) for both you and your partner, and then determine what has to be done in order to buy back additional benefits if these are available to you.

Get form NP 38

Buy back years' service

- If you believe that you will be under-funded at retirement, make the decision now as to whether your fixed assets, properties, investments etc will be solely available to provide for your old age, or whether you wish your dependants or heirs to benefit from your estate. Taking the decision whether to benefit yourself, as opposed to merely preserving your estate for the benefit of your heirs, could give you significant additional options in retirement, should your income be insufficient. This is a major decision for people who feel duty-bound to pass on their wealth after death, as opposed to maximising their capital and income resources for a happy and contented retirement.

Benefit self or heirs?

- Decide to review and examine critically your present insurances, such as car insurance, household insurance, contents insurance, as there are significant savings which may be made through a simple re-broking process, each year, to create more disposable income. I come across cases every day where people are paying up to double what they should be for these coverages. Recently I was speaking to someone who was about to renew their household contents insurance policy and had been quoted an annual premium of £900. A couple of phone calls proved that she could obtain the cover elsewhere for just over £200 per annum! The same applies to life insurance, critical illness cover, health coverages and other benefits.

ACTION

Review coverages

- So that you know exactly where you stand in relation to your present position, ask your employer for a full breakdown of how your pension and other benefits stand at present, and what they are likely to be at retirement. If you are self-employed, or a business owner, ask your financial adviser to complete this exercise for you. You cannot adequately plan unless you know exactly what your present position is.

Get present details of benefits

- If you are divorced, take into account any maintenance arrangements which may continue into retirement, or have to be paid from your estate. Your circumstances may change but that doesn't necessarily mean that your payments will cease. As this affects well over one-third of the population, careful consideration is needed. An ex-spouse could be entitled to a large share of your retirement fund and you may be unaware of this. If contemplating divorce, you may have important decisions to make to preserve your retirement financing as well as estate preservation.

Divorce decisions

- After going through the above check list and decision-making processes, please add any others you feel are important to your circumstances. Make sure you have a full review of your situation completed, either by you or by your financial adviser, so you can effectively plan ahead, knowing exactly what all your options are throughout the accumulation phase prior to actual retirement. Other critical decisions could include whether to remain in the pension funds you're in, whether to change or move your investments for a better return or security, deciding on what type

Better investments

of pension plan is most suitable for you and　　**ACTION**
ascertaining how far your employer is able to　　*Employer*
assist in your financial planning.　　　　　　　*assistance*

By focusing on the above, you can get a clearer idea as to whether you can retire as planned, or take early retirement, or even postpone retiring for a year.

Prioritising what needs to be done means you can now select your critical path in the retirement planning process up to the normal retirement date.

Critical decisions at retirement date

Your decision-making process for the actual act of retirement begins more than a year before your retirement date. This is the period during which you are collecting information on which to base your retirement options, both with a view to income as well as capital growth on your investment portfolio and underlying funds. It is also the time when you will receive a tax-free cash lump sum from your pension scheme and you may have maturing endowment policies and other investments to take into consideration. You will have to decide whether to pay off a mortgage or loans, or whether to reduce these substantially, leaving lower commitments to be covered, and this will be a trade-off between expending capital or income in the long term. Also, one year's notice is often required by pension fund trustees if you are transferring into a Section 32 plan and contemplating the drawdown facility for income.

The following will be the major critical decision-making aspects you may have to consider near or at the actual date of retirement:

- Total value of all pension funds to be　　　**ACTION**
  ascertained for best income and tax-free capital
  options. You should be getting different
  annuity quotes if self-employed or a partner, or
  an employee with a personal pension plan, as　　*Get pension*
  well as someone who has previously been in　　　　*fund*
  one of the schemes which is now paid up. You　　*valuations*
  should be considering the best joint and
  survivor options offered by your current
  pension house or life office, so that you can

compare this against the open-market options available for joint and survivor options (where both you and your spouse will benefit) to a single life with no guarantee option. Go direct to the various annuity houses or contact Annuity Direct or the Annuity Bureau to do the work for you. In fact, I find that Annuity Direct offers a specific service to people intending to retire in the future, keeping them up-to-date with changes in annuity rates, as well as new types of options coming into the marketplace. It is well worth belonging to their service, which should be put down to part of your research programme. It also gets you in the frame of mind and focus necessary for the type of decision-making you will be required to do.

- If you have previously covered your pension scheme with life insurance, do not hesitate to take the highest annuity payable under a single life no guarantee. Should you die, your annuity will die with you, but your life policy will pay out the full amount of your original pension scheme for use by your dependants and heirs.

- You will also have to decide whether to take a tax-free lump sum from your pension scheme and a reduced pension, or whether to take a full pension and no tax-free lump sum. Generally speaking, unless your pension provider is able to provide a high level of escalating annual pension per annum, it will always be preferable to take the tax-free lump sum and to invest that yourself, perhaps for a further voluntary purchase annuity – which is tax-efficient and should provide a greater level of income than a compulsory purchase annuity from a pension scheme provider – or for further investment, or use it to reduce your existing liabilities. The size of your liabilities at retirement will determine what kind of decisions need to be made at that time. For

ACTION
Get annuity quotes

Join an annuity service

Take the best option

Take the tax-free lump sum

Invest at best, or reduce liabilities, or both

example, if you require more cash at retirement to reduce liabilities, then part of your retirement investment programme through your business might be to go for a FURBS (a Funded Unapproved Retirement Benefit Scheme) which can pay out a lump sum in total if required, or some other form of investment funding, such as an endowment policy or a with-profits traded endowment policy which is bought on the open market.

ACTION

Top up with FURBS or other investments

- One aspect of your retirement countdown programme check list which you should consider is the purchase of items you might need for the family or household, such as a motor vehicle to last you into retirement. Perhaps your business can provide you with a car at low cost or as a gift (see page 192).

Consider new purchases for retirement

- You will have to make choices as to how you wish to draw down your income in retirement. It may be that your income from other sources is sufficient to sustain your living requirements and you do not need additional income from your pension funding. You will therefore be in a position to consider drawing down an income from your pension scheme which you can do up to age 75 before taking an annuity, or phasing your income and capital requirements to yourself (see Chapter 6). Only specific types of pension plans are available with such options. If you are an employee in an occupational pension scheme, you will not have this option unless you have a personal account with a group scheme arrangement. Final salary schemes merely pay out a defined benefit from retirement date. It may be possible for you to transfer your fund value from the final salary scheme to a personal pension style arrangement in order to take advantage of drawdown or phased income and capital in retirement, but this is something which has to be broached with your employer *at least a year* before you intend to retire. The history of your

Decide on income drawdown to 75 or phased retirement or annuity only

Get transfer values

Speak to employer

existing occupational scheme needs to be taken into account and you will have to decide whether you would be better off with your employer's pension, or whether it would be better to transfer your fund to a personal pension arrangement which may have more options.

ACTION

- Your chosen retirement age affects whether you choose a pension which escalates in retirement and, if so, by how much it escalates each year. If you are considering earlier retirement and do not require the income, you will have to balance the effects of tax-free growth within the pension fund itself up to, say, age 75, before taking an annuity, against taking an annuity immediately you retire with an escalation option. There is usually no growth in such an annuity and, because the annuity provider has to guarantee the annual escalations, it will offer you a lower rate than usual. It usually takes on average between seven and eight years for the cross-over point to be reached where you would be on the same terms had you effected a level annuity instead of the escalating annuity in retirement. Thus, you would need to weigh up whether you should take a level annuity and rather invest the annuity payments surplus to your requirements each month, and view that against leaving your pension fund to grow to mature in the pension scheme until age 75 or earlier.

Decide on escalation or growth or both

Get figures for level or escalating annuities

- The question of guarantees is an interesting one. The higher the level of guarantee offered, the lower the level of annuity rate you will be able to receive. You, the annuitant, pay for the guarantee at the expense of any income you may receive. Unless you are able to protect your fund, you may well feel that you require such guarantees to ensure that income is paid out by way of the annuity for your lifetime as well as that of your spouse. However, do bear in mind the insured fund option which would

Decide whether you need a guarantee

initially leave you no worse off than if you had selected a joint and survivor annuity payable for two lifetimes, which also had an income-escalating option at the highest level. *This is guaranteed to get you the lowest annuity rate available in the marketplace.* The cost of insuring your fund is made up of the difference in the annuity rate between what you would have taken and what is now being offered to you – a single life no-guarantee annuity from the best open market option annuity provider. You would therefore be no worse off from an *income point of view* through selecting the best option single rate annuity with no guarantee, as well as the insured fund option – as the difference in rate pays your life insurance premium. However, in later years, by using the latter mechanism, you have the option to increase your income significantly and possibly your capital base. You will certainly need to do your sums to see which route is most viable for you and your circumstances. Not everyone will be able to benefit from the insured fund route, unless they are prepared to fund the premium costs from other sources, if too high.

- You should complete a future cash-flow analysis at this time, indicating your monthly expenditures and your future income expectations. This will enable you to plan whether to take the full amount of your pension immediately, or possibly to defer the taking of your pension until a later date. You may also, as a result of this exercise, decide to draw down or phase your retirement income according to your needs. Income drawdown is also a means of preserving your capital within the fund for as long as possible, whilst having use of an income stream provided by that capital, without having to purchase an annuity which *must* be done currently by age 75. You are carefully streamed in respect of how much

ACTION

Consider whether the insured fund route is for you

Get quotes and rates for both options

Draw up a list of your monthly expenses and income requirements

Decide on how much income you need at different phases

income you are able to draw down, so that you do not unnecessarily deplete your pension fund.

ACTION

- You will have to decide when to align the maturity dates of your pension policies, endowment funds and other investments. Some retirees would not wish to have everything maturing at the same time, and would rather see a phasing-in of income and capital as it is required in respect of their cash-flow analysis.

Align maturity dates of investments and funds

- It is important to plan for the investment of these tax-free lump sums coming from pension funds and maturing endowment policies etc. The investment strategy for older people with not much money will have to be fairly conservative, but the more capital you have, the more speculative in higher growth investments you can become. Investment planning is therefore a most important decision-making process, as it will need to be either income or growth oriented, or a mixture of both.

Decide on income or growth investments and your risk profile

- As if all of the above is not enough, the recent retiree will also have to contend with planning his additional free time, organising his social life or possibly changing career direction. All of these social, emotional, leisure and other pursuits will need to be decided on, as well as regular holidays, seeing children and grandchildren and providing gifts for them, possibly moving to a smaller house and having to cope with doing without those business lunches!

Plan what to do with your time in retirement

- Take into account the fact that you may need proper retirement counselling as part of your change of lifestyle. Decide on when and how you are going to do this, and make sure that both you and your partner attend any sessions which are being given in your area.

Get retirement counselling

Post-retirement decision-making

This type of decision-making can be compared to a well-tended garden.

Starting with an empty flowerbed or border, the gardener plants seeds and bulbs at the right time of year, planning carefully, and then waters and nurtures them as they grow to young plants and through to maturity, providing a resplendent display. By constantly tending and enriching the soil, he ensures that the beautiful blooms will grow year after year.

This is also the case with your maintenance and review programme after you have retired. You will have to take further steps to increase the preservation of your capital and income streams, particularly as legislation changes and outside environmental and economic issues may affect your lifestyle.

You should make regular reviews of your investments to ensure that they are performing efficiently, or that you are enjoying the best tax breaks available. Other events could occur – a death, ill health, the demise of your car, a business debt needing to be repaid.

Be prepared!

Your decision-making processes will mostly be confined to the following:

- Review and monitor your investments and take critical and tax-efficient decisions. 'Bed and breakfast' your investments to make use of the annual capital gains tax exemptions, or make tax-efficient investments into Enterprise Zone Trusts or venture capital trust investments (if indeed tax will be a problem); you may wish to move from investments in the building society or with banks (should interest rates fall and your income decrease) towards other investments which may offer guarantees and higher income. Keeping your investment portfolio current is therefore something which should be looked into at least once a year and preferably every six months. *ACTION* — *Review and monitor investments every six months*

- Each time a lifetime event occurs, you will have to make appropriate decisions. Depending on your retirement structure with regard to *Plan for uncertain events*

pensions and annuities, some of these decisions will be automatic, whilst others will need to have various options exercised.

ACTION

- The possibility of going into a residential home or into a more expensive care programme is also something that at least 20% of retirees will have to consider, either for themselves or for their spouse. This leads on to decision-making with regard to the home, future heirs, adequacy of income and capital and advice about how to cope with this situation and its financing (see Chapter 10).

Residential care possibilities

- Estate planning is an important aspect and decisions have to be made. Wills need to be updated and, if required, trusts set up to protect assets with growth potential from inheritance taxes – although this should have been done during the accumulation stage if at all possible.

Update wills

Set up trusts

- The home is probably the most important asset in most people's portfolios, not only as a place to be enjoyed and lived in, but also as investment potential. Should the need arise, there are a number of useful ways to create more income through using the home. These range from safe home income plans to annuity purchase arrangements using the home as security, to equity drawdown arrangements when the house is finally sold, in order to pay back the lender once the retiree has died. These will probably be decisions which need careful consideration and time. If, through your planning and other financial arrangements, you have already decided you may suffer an income shortfall in retirement without using the home, it is best to plan for this eventuality as early as possible. There are numerous strategies which may be employed to enable you to carry on living in your home, yet to use its asset value to give you further income in retirement. For some people, this could mean 50% more income at least.

Consider using the home for more income

- Planning for your dependants also needs to be done. You need to decide how much income and capital will be required by your dependants should you die, and whether what will be provided will be sufficient. You will also need to decide on the levels of protection of this income and capital (possibly through using a trust), and who will assist with administering your estate and your affairs.

ACTION

Plan for income for dependants

- Finally, having spent your lifetime building up your net worth and accumulating wealth, it would almost be criminal to lose at least 40% of it through inheritance taxes on your death because you did not plan properly or take the correct decisions at the time. That is why it is important to have a personal financial plan compiled for you to take you through this entire process in respect of lifestyle planning.

Get a personal financial plan compiled

Whilst there is every possibility that you will change your mind about things as your circumstances alter, at least try to see the road ahead and therefore the potential pitfalls. If you know what they might be, you can plan for them There is no greater heart-attack material than when one of life's great surprises suddenly strikes you in the gut. My friend Elaine had a massive shock. She had assumed that her pension from her employment would keep her adequately provided for until she died. Not so. Within a year of retiring, her daughter and child had moved back in with her and her husband had left her for a younger woman. She had made no provision for retirement, believing that the State and her employer would provide. She ended up having to sell the family home and move into a much smaller house in a different area.

It is always wise to get a second opinion. Although I'm an experienced financial planner, I often seek a second opinion from a fellow financial planner with regard to my advice to my own clients. No one is 100% right 100% of the time. If you take time to consider and reflect, you may well adopt a different course of action or strategy.

No one can make proper planning decisions unless all of the information is to hand. It is for this reason that many people require financial assistance to help them become their own retirement and financial expert.

Key points summary

- This chapter has dealt with the importance of planning a critical decision-making path through the various phases in the retirement process.
- Decisions have to be made during the accumulation phase up to retirement date.
- Critical decisions have to be made at actual retirement date and immediately before that date.
- Lifestyle planning decisions need to be made in the post-retirement period. These may lead to decisions involving the house, going into a home or long-term care, inheritance taxes and other major issues.

Action plan

Construct your own critical path to retirement (and beyond), using as the main action points those given in this chapter.

CHAPTER 6

Selecting the Best Annuity and Pension Options at Retirement

> *An annuity is a very serious business.* **Mrs Dashwood in *Sense and Sensibility* by Jane Austen (1775-1817)**

Objective: To select the best options to enable you to retire comfortably and to increase income as well as capital in retirement years

This chapter signals the crux of all your hard preparatory work towards the funding of your retirement. It is also the most crucial in that decisions made now could well be irreversible. One thing is certain though – you will have the benefit of looking at all the options available to you and then you can make the appropriate decisions as to how you wish to receive your income and build your capital in retirement.

For some, such as most employees in occupational pension schemes, the choices are narrow. Your employer will arrange for your pension payments to commence from retirement date, and you will receive a tax-free lump sum for investment purposes, unless you transfer to a personal pension plan which may offer those options. For those in money purchase schemes, personal pensions and similar plans (such as retirement annuities), the options are greater and require deeper investigation.

Astute investors and their advisers should be able to *increase* future income significantly and preserve capital within pension funds for as long as possible – even for the benefit of succeeding generations.

In my survey of those who have *already* retired, I asked them what they would do if they could do it all again. Hindsight is a marvellous teacher; their comments will possibly give you some idea of how to approach things differently:

- *'Plan to have enough. My biggest worry was not having enough to live on in retirement. As a result, I lead a frugal life, living on the bare necessities only. I'm not afraid of death. What I am afraid of is living in poverty for the rest of my life.'* Bill, now age 81, has been retired for 16 years.

- *'No one could tell me exactly what my options were at the time. Everything was a rush. I think I did my best, with a guaranteed income for me, and for wife after I've gone. Now I'm bitter because my wife died before me – after 43 years of wonderful marriage – and I'm stuck with the same level of income, I suppose, until I die. I believe now I could have done it differently but I didn't know then. Also, these options were not available then.'* Harry, now 77, has been retired since age 60.

- *'I must tell you that I'm not a money person. The life office wrote to me telling me what pension and cash lump sum to take. I thought at the time that it didn't amount to much, but I took it with them. After all, I saved with them for over 35 years – so why not? What I would have done differently is look after me, not them. I didn't know about the open market options and moving funds for better income. No one told me. Even if they had told me, I still needed help to get the best deal.'* Elaine, divorced, retired for 10 years.

- *'What's the point of losing it all to the life office when I die? There must have been a better way – I just didn't know what it was. I'm more concerned now than ever before that my income won't last and I may lose my house. This is very stressful for both of us. Sure, retirement is very nice, except for the constant worry and our deteriorating health. If I could do it again, I definitely would have done something different to keep more of what I had.'* Ben, married, retired over 30 years now.

- *'The business I worked for could have done more. They kept saying we had the best pension scheme and I believed them. After 20 years' service, all I got was 15% of my salary. It was difficult then bringing up a family with nothing left over for more pension funding. Who even thought of it? This is a welfare state, you know. Doing it all over, I wouldn't have been complacent about it – I would have saved something – anything. It would certainly help now.'* Graham, 70, retired 10 years ago.

- *'I would have planned it better. If I knew the options available and considered some of the advice, I know I could have got a better deal. This is what is annoying me – the fact that you only get one bite at the cherry and then you buy the whole tree. I couldn't find anyone I trusted enough to give me proper advice. No one seemed to care when I reached retirement.'* Denis, 67, retired for only two years.

There is certainly plenty of anecdotal evidence to suggest that not planning well in advance, not knowing what options are available, and selecting incorrect options for one's circumstances, all lead to worry and often despair in later life.

That is why it is important to consider the widest range of options so that informed choices can be made. It is also one of the reasons why I developed and formed the first open market option clearing house for pensions and annuities in the UK. I was as frustrated as my clients in not having enough information available to plan adequately.

There is no point in going any further unless you fully understand what pensions and annuities are, how they are constructed and how they can best benefit you.

IF EMPLOYED: OCCUPATIONAL PENSION SCHEMES

If you are employed and a member of an occupational pension scheme, then you have very little choice in respect of your options at retirement. You will retire in accordance with the rules of your pension fund. Generally, these will entitle you to a *pension* based on your years of service with the business, which will be taxable.

You will also qualify for a *tax-free lump sum* which is determined according to a commutation factor (usually 12 times your annual pension). If in a good scheme, there should be widows' and dependants' pensions payable if you should die whilst in retirement.

STRATEGY 54
If in an occupational pension scheme, examine the
rules for your options!

Some schemes are very good, offering wonderful benefits; others may not be so good.

You may wish to make the comparison between your occupational pension scheme and a personal pension retirement plan. You can move your fund's value from your employer to a personal pension plan before retirement if you think you will get a better deal. However, most occupational schemes do offer good value and guaranteed pension benefits and you should only make the move if it is definitely in your favour to do so. After the Maxwell pensions fiasco, some retirees may not want their employers to control their pension destinies; others may find that transferring to the 'private sector', especially if annuity rates are high, is a better bet.

STRATEGY 55
Consider all your options and have the calculations
made for you if on an occupational scheme

If considering options, begin the process *at least* a year before you retire.

Where the occupational pension scheme is in the hands of your employers (who may well use annuities to pay pensions in any event) you have little control; if you are self-employed and have personal pension plans, retirement annuities and money purchase schemes, then *you* will have control as well as a multitude of different choices.

IF YOU HAVE RETIREMENT ANNUITIES, PERSONAL PENSION PLANS OR MONEY PURCHASE ARRANGEMENTS

With these types of plans, you may choose a pension (known as an annuity) only, or a reduced pension (annuity) *and* a tax-free lump sum.

STRATEGY 56
Always choose the tax-free lump sum – it's more tax-efficient

Unless you need the tax-free lump sum to reduce liabilities, pay for your dream holiday, or other capital expenditures, then it can be invested for income. As you will see later in this chapter, there are two types of annuity to purchase – one is based on your *pension fund* and the other is based on your *private capital* as a source. Once you take your tax-free lump sum, it then *becomes* private capital and different annuity rules apply which are more tax-efficient. In other words, by taking your tax-free lump sum in cash and merely purchasing an ordinary annuity (known also as a purchased life annuity, or immediate annuity), this will *increase* your income because a part of that income is not taxable. Ordinary annuities normally offer the best value to people over age 65.

The *balance* of your pension fund will buy you an *annuity* known as a *pension annuity*. The different variations are given below. All annuities will give you the following options to consider, depending upon your needs for flexibility and security, and your fear of loss of capital; whether you should leave a pension for your dependants and how to do so; dealing with inflation eroding your income, and a host of other issues.

Much of this choice is down to your own circumstances and outlook on life and, of course, when you have chosen to retire. It is also down to life expectancy. If you do not expect to live for a substantial period, then your choices may well be different as to how you wish to receive your income.

For example, if you don't have longevity in your family history, then this may be a factor in choosing a *level* annuity as opposed to one which escalates. However, if your normal life expectancy looks like beating the odds, then you may well opt for lower income now, with the expectation of greater income later. This may be the case if you retire early and have considerable years in retirement ahead of you. Remember one thing common to *all* options: the greater the levels of guarantee taken, the greater the cost of providing a guarantee, and therefore the *less* the income available on which to live. This dilemma is a real 'Catch 22' situation. Most people need *increasing income* in retirement and need to squeeze their pension funds for as much as they can get. Guarantees to pay pensions to dependants on your death, escalating annuities, guarantee periods and so on can *reduce* the income available to you now by up to 50%.

In a nutshell, the following will be your options at retirement:

- Take a tax-free lump sum and a reduced pension.   ❏
- Take a full pension only, and no tax-free lump sum.   ❏
- Take a pension guaranteed for your lifetime only.   ❏
- Take a pension guaranteed to pay you and, when you
  die, your widow or widower.   ❏
- As above, but paying a dependant's pension to children as
  well.   ❏
- Take a pension at normal retirement age, *or*   ❏
- Defer taking a pension until you finally have to do so
  at age 75   ❏
  - Drawing down an income from the fund itself only, *or*   ❏
  - Phasing your retirement by taking annuities and tax-free
    cash from time to time.   ❏
- Utilise the open market option for the *best* annuity rates.   ❏
- Choose the income payments and their frequency   ❏
  - in advance   ❏
  - in arrears   ❏
  - each month   ❏
  - each quarter   ❏
  - each half year   ❏
  - each year   ❏
  (The highest income will be annually in arrears, the lowest
  monthly in advance.)
- Have level income, *or*   ❏
- Have escalating income.   ❏
- Have guarantee periods (the annuity continues after your
  death).   ❏
- Choose the type of annuity required
  - Traditional guaranteed income annuity   ❏
  - With profits annuities   ❏
  - Unit linked annuities.   ❏
- If you have a partner, the elder of the two should buy the
  ordinary annuity from tax-free capital. This should give
  a higher level of income.   ❏
- Insure your fund option (Strategy 130 and 131).   ❏

As you can appreciate, everyone will have different circumstances to consider, and therefore the very wide range of options
available may appear confusing. Which do you take? Which do
you avoid? Above all, how do you know that you have done the
right thing? Once your decisions are made, they will be final –
there is no going back. You can't say after a year, 'I made the
wrong choice – I should have deferred my pension, rather than
take an annuity now.' Once your choice has been made, that is it.

Possibly your approach to this wide range of choice is to decide
on the conceptual approach first, then fill in the detail later. This
will make the choice of options easier.

Best income choice – small fund   ❑

- Open market option transfer.
- Single life annuity with or without guarantee (or insure the
  fund if without).
- Income monthly in arrears for monthly; annually in arrears for
  annual.
- Escalate income if life expectancy is on your side.

Best income choice – large fund and no immediate income need   ❑

- Defer retirement date to age 75.
- Fulfil income needs through drawdown of income later, *or*
- Phased retirement options.
- A combination of drawdown and phased options to suit your
  income and capital needs.
- At age 75 you must take an annuity:
  - For guaranteed no-change income take a conventional
    annuity using the open market option.
  - For fluctuating income, but possibility of growth, take a
    with-profits or unit-linked annuity.

You could insure your fund at *normal* retirement date when
younger. If so, then elect the single life no guarantee annuity for
highest income. On your death, your *full original pension fund*
pays out tax-free to your nominated beneficiary.
   Only use escalating income options if at younger retirement
ages and with an expectation of longevity.

Income payments depend on the frequency required. The later you can take income, the higher the level of income. For example, income coming to you yearly in arrears has a higher level than income arising monthly in advance.

Compare the above options to the following which is opting for the most guarantees:

Best safety and guarantee options – lower income   ❏

- Use the open market option for the best annuity rates.
- Choose a joint and survivor annuity (if you have a spouse)
  - which is guaranteed for, say, five years
  - which pays a pension to your spouse
    - at 100% of your pension
    - at 50% of your pension
  - which may escalate in value over time
    - at 3%
    - at 5%
    - at the RPI (retail price index)
  - which is payable monthly in advance.

This scenario is the most common; well over 90% of retirees opt for the best safety and guarantee options. However, there is *always* a trade-off between having guarantees and not having them, and this is reflected in the annuity rate being offered to you.

Those with smaller pension funds who are totally reliant on their pensions, with no other income sources, will, in all likelihood, choose the safety and guarantee options. The *difference* in income between the more flexible, higher income options and the safety options can be as much as 60% and rising over time. Your decisions will be based on your risk profile, the amount of pension fund capital available to you (those with larger amounts can afford to be more flexible) and your personal circumstances.

STRATEGY 57

Get comparative quotations on the different options available to you, depending on your objectives and personal circumstances

---

You owe it to yourself to do this. I have come across too many people just taking what their pension provider offers them. Merely opting for the open market option *only* could increase your income by an *average* of 15%. It may be as high as 60% if annuity rates are low, but an annuity provider is looking for new business, thus offering better rates.

Where you built up your pension fund may not generally provide you with the best pension – always check out the open market option for a better deal.

Ask the questions: Do you want a pension for yourself only, and for your lifetime, or do you want a spouse or dependant to benefit when you die? How do you want to be paid – in advance or at the end of the period? Do you want income monthly, quarterly, six-monthly or annually? Do you want your income to increase each year? If so, by how much? What sort of annuity do you want? Must it be level and guaranteed for life, or can you afford to take the chance of an invested annuity in a unit-linked or with-profits fund, where the income may fluctuate? Do you wish to preserve your retirement capital for your heirs, free of inheritance taxes? Are you in ill-health, or a smoker? If so, you may get even *better* annuity rates as the chances of you living your normal life span are reduced.

It is *vital* that you discuss your retirement options with a qualified retirement planner. Imagine this scenario: for 40 years you scrimped and saved to build up your retirement fund. It has grown well, giving better than average returns. Come retirement day, you make the wrong choices and end up with a mediocre income return on your fund. You could be *losing* up to 60% or more of your income potential by not planning properly – what a waste!

Having considered which options are most suitable for you, you will now wish to know what the various mechanisms are and how they are described and which ones are most suitable for your circumstances.

What is an annuity?

An annuity is an insurance policy which *guarantees* to pay an annual income (the annuity) every year (broken down to suit you as monthly, quarterly, six-monthly or annual payments) for as long as you live, or longer.

You may choose an annuity which continues after your death, to pay your spouse or partner an annuity (or pension) if you prefer.

The level of income payable by an annuity depends on many factors, particularly your age and sex (women tend to live longer than men and as a consequence, their annuity rates are *lower*, as the annuity must pay out for longer). The older you are when you buy your annuity, the higher the level of income you will receive.

There are two main types of annuity:

- *A pension annuity*, which is bought with money from a pension fund. This is known as a *compulsory purchase annuity* and is bought from company pensions, directors or executive schemes, additional voluntary contribution (AVC) plans and small self-administered pension plans (SSASs).
- *An ordinary annuity*, which is bought with private capital. This type of annuity is used to provide an income from your tax-free lump sum, for example. It is more tax-efficient as part of your own private capital is returned to you partly as income. These annuities are also known as purchased life annuities (PLAs), immediate annuities (IAs) or voluntary purchase annuities (VPAs).

The rest of this chapter deals with pension annuities *only.*

The open market option (OMO)

STRATEGY 58
Always investigate the OMO for better income

Most pension funds have what is known as the 'open market option'. This gives you the freedom to buy a pension annuity from any company you choose – so that you can shop around for the best possible income at the time you retire. Annuity rates can vary widely among well-known insurance companies – sometimes the top company can be paying between 40% and 60% more income than the worst one; at other times the difference may be around 15%.

Under the open market option, when you buy your annuity, your pension fund is transferred directly to the chosen annuity supplier which pays out any tax-free cash (if you have opted for this) as well as paying your income for life.

Over four billion pounds' worth of pension funds are being converted to annuities every year as people retire from work. It is therefore important to use a bureau like Annuity Direct to get the best options available for your circumstances.

Tax-free cash

STRATEGY 59
Always take the tax-free cash for more flexibility and better returns

---

When you use the open market option, your tax-free cash amount will be 25% of your fund, whether from a personal pension plan or a retirement annuity plan. If you have retirement annuities maturing, be aware that your tax-free cash amount may decrease from around 33% to 25% – although your pension (annuity) will be greater.

Sometimes it is better to invest your tax-free portion into an *ordinary annuity* for more efficient income. At other times, you may prefer to invest it into a growth investment, choosing your time carefully to take out the annuity. Remember, the older you are, the better the annuity rate.

Annuity rate

The annuity rate is the rate given (or factor) which determines your level of income. It is usually measured in units of either £1,000 or £10,000. The rate may be, say, £80 worth of annuity for every £1,000 invested.

Calculation of the *rate* depends on: age, sex, health (if asking for an impaired life annuity), amount of the annuity, guarantees required (such as whether to pay out for two lifetimes or only one, whether to have a level or escalating annuity and so on), underlying interest rates in the marketplace, the amount of capital being deployed, the income frequency payments, the views of the annuity provider on the investment market, the use of the open market option, and so on.

The annuity rate is *very sensitive* to underlying interest rates in the marketplace and when these move, the annuity rate will also move, either up or down. Over the past two or three years, the value of the annuity rate has fallen by 25-30% as interest rates on gilts have declined.

Timing

STRATEGY 60
Establish whether annuity rates are rising or falling before you act

---

It is most important to have a general investment market overview to establish whether annuity rates are in a rising or falling market. It may pay you to wait for higher rates before taking your annuity, or even to take it early, if interest rates are high at that time with a possibility of falling in the near future.

Annuity rate uncertainty, as well as uncertain investment returns, have made the need for *flexibility* most important, and over the years a number of significant changes have occurred in the pensions retirement market, including traditional inflexible annuities being joined by unit-linked or with-profits annuity products.

We used to say that there was no growth in an annuity itself, making it more advantageous to leave your pension fund intact and growing for as long as possible before taking the annuity option. All of this has now changed and today's retiree is faced with a number of flexible, tax efficient and increased-control choices.

We now not only have 'growth' annuities, but the retiree can choose to either leave his pension fund itself to grow for as long as possible (up to age 75) or to phase his retirement income and tax-free cash as his needs dictate. These new options have been brought about by low interest returns and low annuity rates in the past and this increased flexibility augurs well for the future. The bottom line for you is that it means *more income* in the future, as well as greater flexibility and better options.

WHICH TYPE OF ANNUITY IS BEST FOR YOU?

STRATEGY 61
Examine the different options carefully before deciding which annuity type and structure is best for your future income

---

Before the different alternatives to buying a traditional pensions annuity are examined, the different types of annuity available to you will be considered.

Single life annuity

This type of annuity is only payable for your lifetime and then it ceases. It will pay the highest income but, when you die, it stops. If you have a partner, you may wish to consider a joint life annuity, or utilising the 'insured funds' option, or other alternatives.

Joint life annuity

This type of annuity pays out for two lifetimes. As a result, it pays out a lower income than a single life annuity. If you die first, an income is paid to your partner for his or her lifetime. You can choose how much income your partner will get if you die first – it could be 100% of the joint income paid by the annuity, but usually it is two-thirds of that amount, or lower, such as 50%.

The major problem here is that, if your partner *dies before you*, you are still locked into a lower income for the rest of your life.

Level or escalating annuities

A level annuity provides the same level of income throughout your lifetime. It will never go up. With this option, you run the risk of being caught out by inflation. During your working life, your pay normally increases to cope with rises in the cost of living. A level pension or annuity cannot provide this facility. An escalating annuity can – but comes with its own dilemmas.

STRATEGY 62
Only choose an escalating annuity if time is on your side and you can manage with less income initially

---

Escalating annuity

With this option, you can decide whether you need your income to escalate in retirement or not. Usually the escalating annuity increases are at 3%, 5% or in line with the retail price index, which gives an index-linked income.

Income from an escalating annuity will start off on a *lower* income than a level annuity. Usually it takes about 8 to 10 years for an escalating income to catch up with the amount of income paid from a level annuity.

A number of factors will influence your choice in opting for an escalating annuity:

- *Timing of the annuity.* If taken at a younger age, there is more chance of experiencing increasing returns later on. It is unlikely that an annuitant at age 75 will take an escalating annuity. If he or she dies within 10 years, then a level annuity would have been better.
- *Life expectancy.* Don't take an escalating annuity if in ill health or with a family history of low life expectancy.
- *Amount of fund available.* If you need more income (not less) in the short term, then don't take an escalating annuity. This type of annuity option will usually only be taken by those who can afford to wait for increasing income at a later date.

If you can afford it – think again. Can you get a better return on your surplus funds than 3%, 5% or the RPI? Perhaps you would be better off taking the level annuity and *investing* any income surplus to your requirements, thus giving you another capital lump sum in 10 years' time. This could then be applied to a Purchased Life Annuity, using your own capital, at an even higher rate, as you will be 10 years older.

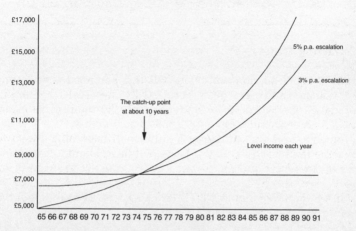

LEVEL v. ESCALATING ANNUAL INCOME
£100,000 joint life annuity, male aged 65,
female aged 60, two-thirds spouse's pension

Source: Annuity Direct, December 1995

STRATEGY 63
Consider an investment-linked annuity if you can accept the risk of fluctuating income

---

With-profits annuities and unit-linked annuities are available for those who can afford to take a chance of fluctuating annuity incomes. You don't have to buy an annuity where your income is fixed from the outset. You can choose an annuity which depends on the growth of funds invested in the stock market. *The income paid to you can go up or down* depending on the performance of the funds you choose.

With-profits annuities

These are most popular because the smoothing effect of bonuses avoids major short-term fluctuations and provides a more stable income stream.

The argument for annuitants is: why lock yourself into fixed interest investments (the level annuity) when the period in

retirement may be as long as, or longer than, the period in which
the pension fund was building up.

Since May 1996 the stock market has *risen* by over 10% (to March
1997) whilst annuity rates have *fallen* by about 3% over the same
period. There has been a fall in annuity rates of some 25% since
1990 (to March 1997), yet equities have increased by over double
the rate at which annuity rates have fallen. Whilst higher interest
rates may occur in the future, you need to keep a careful eye on the
stock market if you wish to maximise your pension income.

Yet, well over 90% of annuitants lock themselves into fixed
income annuities, unwilling to take the chance of fluctuating
incomes in retirement. Investment-linked annuities have only
been available for the last 10 years as an open market option when
Equitable Life launched their unit-linked and with-profits
annuities. A number of annuity offices now offer unit-linked and
with-profits annuity contracts, yet they have been slow to take off.
With-profits annuities are best suited to those who are prepared to
take the investment risk associated with equity investments and
who appreciate that, in the long run, equities should produce
higher returns than a conventional gilt-based annuity.

Generally, it is better to secure a fixed interest (level) annuity
when annuity rates are high and consider buying with-profits
annuities when rates are low.

Investment-linked annuities are structured in exactly the same
way as conventional annuities, with the exception that, instead of
providing a guaranteed income, the value of future payments will
fluctuate, depending on investment returns.

With investment-linked annuities, the income payments are recal-
culated each year and are dependent on the value of the underlying
fund. On the other hand, conventional annuity payments are fixed
and guaranteed from the outset for the lifetime of the annuitant.

STRATEGY 64
Compare investment-linked to conventional annuities
before making your choice

COMPARISON OF WITH-PROFIT ANNUITIES AND CONVENTIONAL
ANNUITIES

Joint annuity, £100,000 purchase, male aged 60, female aged 57, guaranteed 5 years, 2/3 widows paid monthly. With profits annuities assume 9% investment growth less charges.

With-profit annuities

Anticipated bonus	3% p.a. £	5% p.a. £	7% p.a. £
Annuity in year 1	5,528	6,864	8,266
Annuity in year 5	6,698	7,554	8,277
Annuity in year 10	8,415	8,621	8,596
Annuity in year 15	10,573	9,838	8,927
Annuity in year 20	13,285	11,229	9,271

- The higher the anticipated bonus, the higher the starting income.
- The rate of future growth is higher where a *smaller* anticipated bonus is chosen.

Conventional annuities

Escalation	5% p.a. £	3% p.a. £	Level £
Annuity in year 1	5,327	6,650	8,861
Annuity in year 5	6,475	7,485	8,861
Annuity in year 10	8,264	8,677	8,861
Annuity in year 15	10,547	10,059	8,861
Annuity in year 20	13,461	11,661	8,861

- Shows income from three types of conventional annuity, two escalating and one level.
- The 5% escalating annuity is similar to the with-profits annuity with a bonus projection of 3%; the 3% escalating annuity is similar to the with-profits annuity with a bonus projection of 5%.

Source: Annuity Direct

The maximum with-profit anticipated bonus is 7% p.a. and this is 10% lower than the level annuity. Care should always be taken when making comparisons, due to the different starting points in annuity rates and investment returns able to be earned. Wherever *you* are in the investment-annuity cycle, have the figures calculated for you. Like any growth versus fixed interest investments, the likelihood of being ahead over longer terms usually lies with growth investments. There again, higher ages could get much higher annuity rates, as could impaired lives.

What would significantly swing with-profits and unit-linked annuity investments in favour of annuitants would be if the value of the with-profits fund was transferable in full to heirs on death, as in South Africa.

In the UK, there is much scope for innovation. Return of funds on death is one example. Another would be protected capital annuities, similar to stock market tracker funds where most of the upside growth is captured, but the downside loss on falling markets is ignored. The most balanced would be an investment-linked annuity which provided a guaranteed lifetime income with the potential for long-term growth.

Guarantees on annuities

Guarantee periods can be purchased to ensure 'value for money' should you die shortly after purchasing your annuity. This option is expensive; however, if death occurs during the guarantee period, then income would continue to be paid to your estate or to a nominated beneficiary until the end of the guarantee period. Note, however, that including *any* guarantee *reduces* your income from the annuity.

Impaired life annuities

STRATEGY 65
Apply for an impaired life annuity quote if in poor health or a smoker

---

If you are not in good health, have a life-threatening illness, have had a major operation, or are a smoker, then you should apply for an impaired life annuity.

Take the case of Malcolm Williamson: not only was he a smoker, but he weighed nearly 20 stone, was six foot two inches in height, and had experienced high blood pressure for the past 20 years. He had invasive cancer of the lung eight years previously and was considered as uninsurable by life offices. When he reached his retirement age of 70, his pensions annuity provider would only offer him a standard-rated annuity of £12,760. However, the Pension Annuity Friendly Society was able to enhance this by over 50% to £21,002 per annum. Why? Because his life expectancy was much less as a result of his medical condition and lifestyle.

Impaired life annuities are best suited to single lives or joint lives where the spouse's benefit is less than 50%. Of the £4-5 billion annual annuity market, about 10% represents impaired lives, but the figure would be higher if more people knew about this option. Many impaired lives simply accept standard-rated annuities without enquiring further. If you feel you won't make the Queen's birthday telegram (or even come within several years of it) and you have a history of poor or impaired health, then enquire about an impaired life annuity.

The following table shows the enhancements given by the Pension Annuity Society. This is based on a single life annuity, purchase price £50,000, no guarantee, paid level, monthly.

SAMPLE ENHANCED ANNUITY RATES

Life expectancy	Medical condition	Male 60 £	Female 60 £	Male 65 £	Female 65 £
Less than 2 years	Inoperable cancer	44,911	45,060	44,806	44,944
2-5 years	Alzheimer's disease	19,459	19,509	19,410	19,451
5-8 years	Cirrhosis (liver)	12,712	12,729	12,684	12,688
7-10 years	Emphysema	10,773	10,802	10,722	10,746
9-13 years	Non-Hodgkin's Lymphoma	8,558	8,536	8,550	8,506
13-15 years	Diabetes mellitus	7,822	7,820	7,781	7,763
15-18 years	Bronchitis (chronic)	6,216	6,072	6,316	6,117
17-20 years	Hypertension	5,905	5,781	5,974	5,796
	STANDARD ANNUITY	5,258	4,854	5,828	5,242

Source: Money Management, July 1996.

Having an impaired life means more income for you from your pension fund capital. You can also purchase an ordinary annuity from private capital, but the annuity rates may not be the same as a compulsory purchase annuity from a pension fund – in fact, they will probably be less.

STRATEGY 66
The greater the guarantee, the less the income.
Examine all the alternatives before choosing

The impact of different types of annuities, guarantees, frequency or otherwise of payments, impaired lives, use of the open market option or not and the other factors previously mentioned are shown below in respect of *the amount of income* to be expected.

Example of income flows
Male aged 65, female aged 65. Fund available after tax-free cash is £60,000. Payments monthly in advance. All joint life annuities are guaranteed for five years.

	£ per annum	
Best open market option single life, no guarantee, level	**8,340**	**13.9%**
Impaired life	11,590	19.30%
Single life, no guarantee, level	6,685	11.14%
Single life, guaranteed 5 years	6,536	10.89%
Single life, guaranteed 10 years	6,174	10.29%
Joint life, level, 50% spouse pension	5,847	9.75%
Joint life, level, 67% spouse pension	5,671	9.45%
Single life, no guarantee, 3% escalating	5,389	8.98%
Joint life, level, 100% spouse pension	5,320	8.87%
Single life, guaranteed 5 years, 3% escalating	5,276	8.79%
Joint life, 50% spouse pension, 3% escalating	4,602	7.67%
Single life, no guarantee, 5% escalating	4,594	7.66%
Single life, 5 year guarantee, RPI escalating	4,556	7.59%
Single life, 5 year guarantee, 5% escalating	4,513	7.52%
Joint life, 67% spouse pension, 3% escalating	4,414	7.36%
Joint life, 100% spouse pension, 3% escalating	4,802	6.80%
Joint life, 50% spouse pension, RPI escalating	3,896	6.49%

	£ per annum	
Best open market option single life, no guarantee, level	**8,340**	**13.9%**
Joint life, 50% spouse pension, 5% escalating	3,842	6.40%
Joint life 67% spouse pension, RPI escalating	3,732	6.22%
Joint life, 67% spouse pension, 5% escalating	3,661	6.10%
Joint life, 100% spouse pension, RPI escalating	3,444	5.74%
Joint life, 100% spouse pension, 5% escalating	3,347	5.58%
Worst pension provider, joint life, 100% spouse pension, 5% escalating	**2,243**	**3.74%**

The above scenario is where annuity figures have been taken from a reasonably-priced annuity provider. The best open market option reflected a 13.9% amount of income possible at the top end, whereas the worst pension provider only gave a 3.74% return on the £60,000 capital in the pension fund.

The total difference in income in our table from the *same* annuity provider is (£6,685 −£3,347) £3,338 or a difference of 49.93% in income! The difference in open market option shift from the joint life, 100% spouse pension, 5% escalating annuity of £3,347 per annum to the single life, no guarantee, level annuity of £8,340 is 59.87% more income.

This is not to say that everyone should immediately move to the level of greater income. However, what they should do is consider the return on their pension fund capital and their own particular circumstances, and then act accordingly. Insuring the fund and taking the highest annuity possible may be one alternative – another is to opt for albeit fluctuating income from a with-profits annuity or, lastly, to choose the option from the table which you feel most comfortable with.

Remember, once your choice is made, you are locked into that decision for ever.

STRATEGY 67
Even with guarantees, the OMO can usually uplift your income. Always get a quote

---

If you wish to stick with the various guarantees available, then at least consider the open market option. On average, it can increase your income by at least 11%. Sometimes much higher amounts are possible (up to 60% if you move from a 'heavy guarantee' area to one with fewer guarantees).

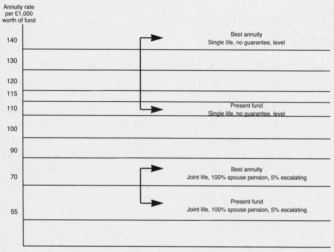

OPEN MARKET OPTION SHIFT

Annuity rate per £1,000 worth of fund

140 — Best annuity
Single life, no guarantee, level

130

120

115

110 — Present fund
Single life, no guarantee, level

100

90

70 — Best annuity
Joint life, 100% spouse pension, 5% escalating

55 — Present fund
Joint life, 100% spouse pension, 5% escalating

Options

In this case, the open market option enables 21% more income to arise for the *same option* where it is the joint life with a 100% spouse pension, escalating at 5% per annum. The shift is similar for the single life, level annuity but with no guarantee. However, it is most dramatic when the shift is from your present fund's joint life, 100% spouse pension with a 5% escalation to the best single life, level, no guarantee option at over 60%.

You may well opt for the nil guarantee option if you have *existing* life cover for your fund value or intend to cover it now. That gives you the *flexibility* to do without costly guarantees and significantly increase your income.

Manipulating annuity rates to choose the best option is one way of seeking greater income potential. However, apart from investment-linked annuities, there is no growth in the annuity itself. The longer you leave your money in the pension fund, the greater the size of your pension fund will become; not only will it grow, compounding each year, but you will also be getting older. This is no bad thing where annuities are concerned. The older you are, the better the annuity rate you can achieve.

STRATEGY 68
Study the options before choosing your retirement plan route

CONVENTIONAL ANNUITIES. PENSION INCOME DRAWDOWN, OR PHASED RETIREMENT?

Whilst you may take a conventional annuity at any age between 50 and 75 from a pension fund (earlier and later if using your private capital), both pension drawdown and phased retirement are flexibility options allowing you to keep your pension fund open and growing for as long as it suits you to do so, but before age 75 at the latest. You may even end up with a hybrid scheme incorporating pension drawdown and phased options, but both will make use of conventional annuities at some stage in the process.

Compulsory purchase annuities

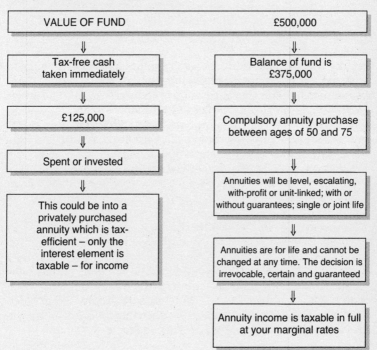

- Immediate retirement action, not gradual.
- No flexibility – once taken you cannot change.
- Unless with-profit or unit-linked annuities, no growth.
- Cost of guarantees is expensive.
- Full tax-free cash must be taken, if required, when the annuity is taken.
- Expectation of greater life expectancy.
- A wager with the life office on how long you will live.
- No real way of increasing income (unless a with-profit or unit-linked annuity, where this *may* be possible).
- Female lives are penalised by at least five years.
- Once taken, on death, or after the guarantee periods, capital and income is lost to the life office annuity provider.
- Will not allow any investment risk (unless investment-linked annuities).
- Some good pension fund managers do not offer annuities.
- Annuity rates may fluctuate or be depressed and you may not get the best deal at the time
- If your spouse or partner dies before you, you could be locked into the lowest income for the rest of your life. Joint life annuities are generally considered to be poor value. Age differentials between spouses also contribute to much lower incomes.

In response to campaigning from life offices such as Winterthur to address the problem of declining annuity rates (they fell from around 15.5% in 1990 to less than 10.5% in 1994) and the lock-in features of conventional annuities, the government eventually announced details of a new pension drawdown facility in the 1994 budget.

Pension income withdrawn

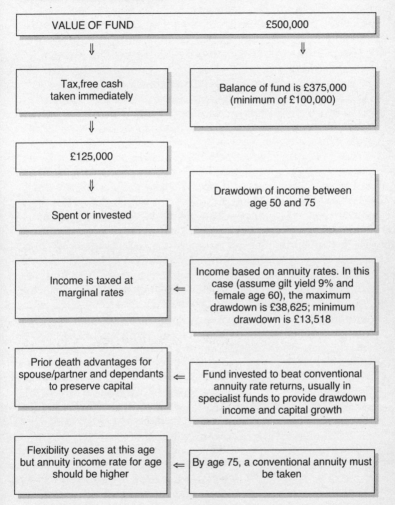

The key features of pension fund drawdown are that the retiree can draw down income from his pension fund as if he had retired, and at a rate of drawdown similar to an annuity. The retiree would then not only have greater control over his or her annuity payments, but also of the underlying investments. Both the income and investment strategy can be changed to reflect the annuitant's changing circumstances.

The new rules allow a person with a personal pension to retire and defer the purchasing of an annuity until his or her 75th birthday. In the meantime, an income may be withdrawn direct from the pension fund. (SSAS arrangements already had this deferment to age 75 from 1993, so the concept was not new.)

Whilst drawing down income in a controlled manner, the retiree can benefit from investment growth. This cannot happen with a conventional annuity when income is fixed (even if it escalates).

Drawdown allows income to be streamed between an upper and a lower limit. The pension income can be paid as frequently as your needs dictate, and the Government Actuaries Department (GAD) produces a table of annuity rates which define the upper income limit. (See Appendix 1 for tables of maximum income withdrawal.)

Each year's pension must be no greater than the upper limit and not less than 35% of the limit. The income taken each year can vary as long as it remains between the two limits. The limits are reviewed every three years to allow for increased age and current gilt yield.

The most *significant advantages* are the death benefits. If the member dies before age 75, then the surviving partner can benefit from the remaining pension fund. The surviving dependant has three options:

- To continue to receive an income in the same way as the original retiree until the policyholder would have attained age 75 or the dependant's 75th birthday if sooner. Dependant children under age 18 can also benefit.

- To receive the balance of the pension fund as a cash sum less a 35% tax charge. At present there is no inheritance tax liability on this amount, unless it is left to the estate. The option must be taken up within two years of the deceased passing away.

- To purchase an annuity for the spouse and/or dependants. If the spouse inheriting the pension fund then dies, the fund can be passed on to heirs.

Under a conventional annuity, on death of the annuitant, the survivor may receive a pension or a reduced pension or no pension, depending on the type of annuity taken, and if there are any guarantees. Pension income withdrawal can defer the eventual taking of an annuity until age 75. Until then, the fund continues to grow free of tax. If one of the aims of pension drawdown is to provide a better return than an annuity then, by definition, the pension fund must be invested in assets that will outperform gilts. This presents a dilemma in that equities in the long run will outperform gilts, but many older people will find the risk unacceptable.

Thus, drawdown is only suitable for those people who have considerable assets outside their pension fund, who will not be left exposed if there is a sudden fall in the value of their pension fund. Drawdown is best suited to keeping retirement options open and preserving capital, possibly at the cost of a reduced income.

Future retirees must be aware of the investment risks in taking income drawdown from their pension funds. For one, the capital of the pension fund may be eroded; future investment returns are uncertain and may not adequately compensate for the capital withdrawn from the fund. Ultimately, withdrawals may provide lower benefits than those from a conventional annuity. No one can predict future gilt rates, and annuities may be at a low level by age 75 when you have to take your annuity.

To make deferral worthwhile, investment returns must make good the shortfall of the withdrawals, whilst at least equalling the amount that an annuity would have provided. Income drawdown is less attractive the older the retiree is, as larger drawdowns are required to match the annuity, which provides a higher income for the older annuitant.

At present, income withdrawal can only take place from a personal pension plan:

Retirement annuity contract (Section 226)	Section 32 Contract or Bond	Free standing AVC	Occupational pension Scheme
⇓	⇓	⇓	⇓

Personal Pension Plan

⇓

Income drawdown facility

However, proposals for introducing drawdown from occupational schemes are well advanced.

Once drawdown starts, the retiree cannot change the provider of the scheme until such time as an annuity is taken. The whole process is, in fact, a complex one of risk management. One has to be careful to take only the fruits of the investment and not to deplete the investment itself. A structured and planned investment approach is therefore essential for success. It is also important to note that once withdrawal starts, no more contributions may be made into this particular fund. In addition, *before* income payments start, the tax-free cash element must be taken – no further tax-free cash may be taken once income payments start. At present, during the period of annuity deferment, the fund, including new investment income, continues to roll up free of income and capital gains tax. This income is taxed in your hands.

STRATEGY 69
Choose a SIPP for maximum investment flexibility

Once income withdrawal has been selected, a transfer of funds to another personal pensions provider is not permitted. Therefore, the choice of pension fund investment vehicle is crucial, as well as the fact that a larger pension fund must be produced with a return significantly greater than the gilt (government security) yields upon which annuity rates are based. The fund will therefore be weighted towards equities or similar risk investments.

Possibly the most suitable investment vehicle is a SIPP (a self-invested personal pension plan). If a SIPP is not used, then the investor could be locked into one fund manager for up to 25 years. Only a SIPP offers the investment flexibility demanded by income withdrawal. As only personal pension plans at present may have income withdrawal, transfers from retirement annuities, money purchase schemes and other types of scheme to a personal pension plan must be made first. A fund of at least £100,000 is required for income drawdown. The SIPP enables the investor to tailor-make his investment portfolio instead of having an insurance packaged fund. For example, Winterthur (the first proponent of SIPPs) has a lower charging SIPP which can invest in a wide range of investments, including equities, unit trusts, investment trusts, government securities, deposits, collective investments and commercial property.

STRATEGY 70

Go for capital protected and guaranteed growth funds to protect from annuity rate falls

---

It is possible to have a guaranteed fund in the drawdown portfolio. There are two types – the rolling fund and guaranteed annuity funds. The rolling funds offer equity exposure with underlying guarantees. The 100% funds have typically returned around 6.5% a year and the 98% funds between 8.5% and 9% a year from launch.

Guaranteed annuity funds provide a guaranteed minimum annuity starting at the end of the term of the investment instead of providing a minimum guaranteed lump sum. To this is added FT-SE 100 growth in the same way as with the traditional guaranteed fund.

As a result, the investor has the potential of equity growth and protection from annuity rate falls.

Take the example of Harry, now aged 63, who has a self-invested personal pension plan (SIPP) worth £500,000. Harry does not wish to retire fully. He will continue to work as a consultant until age 70, when he will retire. Income drawdown seems like the ideal route for him. He opts for the maximum tax-free 25% cash of £125,000 and to take minimum drawdowns to supplement his earnings. The minimum drawdown figure is £13,781.25 per year.

A combined strategy of deposit, three-monthly rolling and three year guaranteed annuity fund will support the minimum drawdown throughout Harry's retirement. The guaranteed funds also provide potential equity growth on top of minimum guarantees. At least £200,000 of his £375,000 remaining fund is still invested in a mixed portfolio of equities to provide longer- term growth to boost the fund when Harry retires fully.

His investment strategy included keeping part of his portfolio liquid for the first few years and the deposit fund was used to provide for the first year's drawdown. The three-month rolling fund investment was used for the second and third year's drawdowns (with a 98% capital guarantee). From year three onwards, the three year guaranteed annuity fund would provide a minimum guaranteed annuity of £14,000 a year, plus any FT-SE growth over the three years.

STRATEGY 71
Choose a specialist fund manager with the correct investment strategy to model your income flows

---

This is a highly complex area of fund management requiring computer modelling and specialist funds to counter the effect of future falling annuity rates, to enhance prospects for fund growth and capital appreciation, and to provide for capital protection where possible. Like Winterthur, Save & Prosper has developed a specialist Retirement Income Fund (theirs invests in a portfolio of cash, gilt-edged securities, equity derivatives and funds which invest in such assets), as have a few other companies. There is no doubt that the investment strategy is the single most important element of the drawdown facility. Drawdown is only recommended if you have considerable assets over and above your pension assets and can afford, if necessary, to live off other income if investment returns are low.

Phased retirement

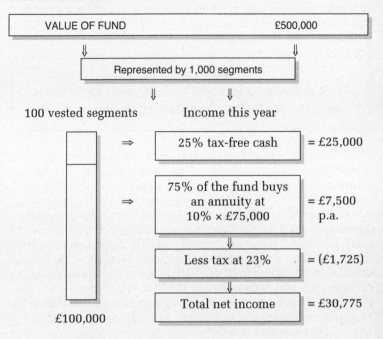

The process is repeated up to age 75, when the final vesting occurs

Phased retirement is a process which involves the gradual encashment of your pension fund. In order to do this, you require a personal pension policy which is written as a number of individual segments, usually 1,000 of them.

Segments are encashed as more capital and income are required in retirement. From each segment, 25% is taken in tax-free cash and the balance of 75% used to purchase an annuity.

In subsequent years the annuity income from the previous encashment continues, whilst new segments can be encashed and the process repeated.

This method is extremely tax and income-efficient as tax payable can be kept as low as possible, whilst income and capital are streamed to take care of need requirements.

The balance of the pension fund is left to grow tax-free until final retirement date, not only keeping available options flexible, but also opting for the prospect of higher annuity rates later on.

The advantages of phasing your retirement income and capital are numerous:

- A gradual retirement is possible.
- There is no need for immediate total tax-free cash.
- There is no need for a total immediate income requirement.
- Income levels can be varied.
- Flexibility allows you to keep your options open.
- There is greater tax efficiency as income includes a high proportion of tax-free cash.
- There is flexibility in the types of annuities purchased. For example, there can be a combination of level and escalating annuities early on if income requirements are low.
- Phasing provides for time to wait for better annuity rates.
- Gradual annuity purchase provides an averaging effect to offset lower annuity rates at certain times.
- The use of the open market option to transfer your fund ensures even better annuity rates.
- There are better annuity rate possibilities – rates for older ages increase with age.
- There is potential to *increase income significantly*, the more so with better fund performance and higher annuity rates.
- There is flexibility to use different annuity providers each time.
- There are *increased death benefits* as remaining policy segments can be used to provide capital, in trust, free of inheritance tax, for beneficiaries. This is an important advantage over the drawdown facility.

Remember, however, that there are also disadvantages in 'staggered vesting' or phased retirement, such as not being able to take 100% of the tax-free cash unless all segments are encashed. Also, lower investment returns could reduce future expected income, and the need for income when annuity rates are low could occur – especially during a period of falling annuity rates, such as 1994 through to 1997. Once purchased, annuities become inflexible and cannot be changed.

As with income drawdown, phased retirement needs a careful strategy with regard to proposed vesting dates when income and capital are required, as well as to underlying investments being made. Whilst the most popular pension plans are still those packaged by the life offices, more and more SIPPs with their flexible structures are being set up to receive transfers from other funds and to consolidate existing plans.

STRATEGY 72
Consider phased retirement for a gradual rise in annuity income and tax-free cash up to age 75

The phased option should be considered for its flexibility, investment control, choice of annuity purchase and timing, as well as the ability to spread the purchasing of annuities. One can also maximise the opportunities for inheritance tax planning and there are greater benefits for dependants. However, the concept of flexibility could be undermined by excessive fund withdrawals which result in a reduced annuity income by comparison with conventional annuities at age 75.

The difference between income drawdown and phased retirement is that under the latter, annuities must be purchased. As the tax-free cash is taken at the same time as the annuities, phased retirement is not an option if tax-free cash is required at final retirement date.

Phased retirement is usually considered suitable for funds of at least £100,000.

COMPARISON BETWEEN ANNUITY, DRAWDOWN AND PHASED OPTIONS

Item	Annuity	Income drawdown	Phased retirement
Description	The pension fund is invested in gilts and fixed interest to pay a guaranteed income for life.	The pension remains invested and the annuity is deferred until age 75. An income is paid from the fund within certain limits.	Each period a segment of the pension is encashed or vested to provide tax-free cash and an annuity. Both together provide income for that year.
The fund	Different annuities may be taken, such as level, escalating or with-profit.	One fund, several withdrawals.	Several separate personal pensions or many segments.

Item	Annuity	Income drawdown	Phased retirement
Tax-free cash	Tax-free cash may purchase a private annuity (PLA) which is tax-efficient for income.	Tax-free cash available in total immediately.	Tax-free cash taken with each segment.
Minimum income	No specific minimum.	Minimum income withdrawal is 35% of the maximum.	No specific minimum.
Maximum income	Highest level of income payable for life, with guarantees.	Maximum income could deplete the pension fund. No guarantees. Annuity purchase by age 75.	Level of income depends on vesting amount. If too high, it could deplete the fund by age 75.
Income flexibility	None.	Income drawdown can be changed each year within limits.	Most flexible option. Each year's income depends on the amount of pension encashed.
Escalation	3%, 5% or RPI.	Limited by expectation of future fund growth and within GAD limits.	Phased annuities can be bought with escalation.
Age	Best suited to over-60's.	Best suited to younger ages. After age 65, more risky than an annuity.	Best suited to younger ages. After age 65, more risky than an annuity.
Term	Age 50-75.	Age 50-75.	Age 50-75.
Investment risk	None on conventional annuities. Unit-linked and with-profit annuities are not guaranteed and will fluctuate.	Investment risk in the pension fund will vary according to the investment strategy and use of guaranteed funds.	More volatility is possible if units have to be sold if the price is low. Otherwise same as for drawdown.

Item	Annuity	Income drawdown	Phased retirement
Death benefits	Annuities can be guaranteed up to 10 years. Joint life annuities pay out for two lifetimes. Unless insured, the underlying fund is lost on death to the life office.	Three options for spouse: • Return of fund less 35% tax; • Remaining fund buys single annuity; • Continue with income withdrawals for two years.	On death, full fund can be paid to dependants free of tax. If transfer originally from a company scheme, then only 25% tax-free cash and balance as annuity.
Health	Most suited if in good health. Impaired life annuities for the seriously ill or smokers.	If pension not required, consider death benefits as better than annuity.	Death benefits better than drawdown. Can also buy impaired life annuities.
Tax	Annuities taxed as Schedule E. Voluntary purchase annuities have a tax-free capital element.	Income taxable as Schedule E.	Very tax-efficient as tax-free cash is used to provide income, thus tax is only paid on the annuity.
Investment amount	Any.	£50,000 to £100,000 fund value minimum.	£100,000 fund value minimum.

STRATEGY 73
Make sure you get best advice when considering all of your option routes

---

The complexity of the different options will make it difficult for financial advisers to give best advice in this crucial area of retirement planning. They must consider not only the options, but also the personal circumstances of their clients (such as life expectancy, health), the financial position of their clients (assets, need for income and tax-free cash), and tax issues, plus other areas such as attitude to risk, inflation, investment choices and strategies, costs of operating the income withdrawal facility and paying advisers.

STRATEGY 74
Position yourself for maximum flexibility to cope with changes in circumstances

---

It is as well to reflect on the decline of State pensions and the increasing dependency of the aged. Between now and the year 2031 the number of pensioners will have increased by more than 50%. People are living longer – in 1952 the Queen issued 210 telegrams to the latest batch of new centenarians; some 43 years later, this figure had increased to 2,750.

Early in 1997 the Tory government announced the privatisation of old age or State pensions. Since then, the new Labour government has come to power and reinforced State pension ideals with a compulsory second tier plan for most workers. This is another message to the consumer to make the most of your investments and income opportunities. It may take years for government plans to become operative, and they may not have any realistic effect on your own retirement plans.

Following the July 1997 budget, the government announced a comprehensive review of pension provision. The Office of Fair Trading brought out its own three-volume report at the same time.

The government review and the OFT report both centred on the fact that people need to save more for retirement income. The government is committed in its nine-point 'challenge' on pensions to a new stakeholder pension that will be 'secure, flexible and value for money'. The government also wishes to narrow the gap between men and women for annuity provision – women receive less.

The OFT report suggests a simple pension invested in index-tracking funds at low cost and compulsory employer contributions, with unisex annuity rates.

Both the government review and the OFT report are aimed at cheap, portable pension (cheaper and simpler than existing personal pension plans) to supplement the existing basic pension and SERPS (the additional State Earnings Related Pension Scheme), this to be the so-called stakeholder pension. The government is expected to call for compulsory savings for retirement. In exchange it will offer tax benefits and low charges. Hopefully, the proposed new model with its risk-controlled growth and low costs will be a sensible mix, but there are many questions to be answered, the least of which is connected with investment performance. The OFT recommendation of only using tracker funds may be a too narrow investment vehicle for better performance, for example.

Purely from a well-intentioned platform the OFT recommendations, highlighting the need that annuities be linked to inflation, that men and women receive equal annuities (women are worse off in both annuity purchase – because they statistically live longer – and income drawdown (see Appendix 1)) is to be commended. This ties in with the government's proposals for unisex annuities, and their overall desire for pension reform. These reforms will encompass certainty in long-term pension funding; fair funding between the state, employer, employee and self-employed; dealing with an ageing population where the ratio of workers to retired people falls; ensuring that everyone's retirement needs are fulfilled; pensions regulation; and ensuring security in retirement for women. All of these proposals are laudable and welcome.

However, what they say and what they do are two different things. The July budget is evidence of that. At the same time as commencing sweeping review proposals, the government abolished tax credits on dividends accruing to equities held by pension funds. Not only will this mean increased funding for employers (estimated at £50 bn), but a general investment performance loss averaged at about 12-15% of fund values. Millions of people with personal pension plans or company money purchase schemes will see their funds grow more slowly, with a fall in real terms of their pensions by up to 15%. The prohibition on pension funds being able to reclaim the tax credit on dividends will result in a fall of pension scheme income from UK equities of 20%. This equates to an approximate reduction in the rate of return on such equities of 0.75% a year.

The obvious implication is that individuals and employers will have to increase their contribution levels radically (by at least 15%) in order to stay level in performance terms. Many may now take the view that locking up funds for a considerable length of time, with inflexible restrictions on how and when to take an annuity or pension, and with lower expected performance, is not for them. They may well look to diversifying into other better-performing investments, such as PEPs, which will continue to benefit from tax credits at least until 5 April 1999.

Coupled with this, possible compulsory funding for a stake-holder pension as advocated by the government will have the effect of employers contributing the bare minimum possible. Far from co-operating with the government review proposals, employers will now critically examine their voluntary funding and some may even downsize their pension funds, rather than take on the burden of increasing contributions.

The way in which investments are structured will also change. Equities will be for growth, whilst gilts and bonds will be preferred for income. Gilts are fine with low inflation, but poor performing gilt yields have visibly kept annuity rates down. The types of annuities available may also change. Those linked to equities for income (which will suffer a 20% reduction) are now going to be critically examined against gilt-based annuities. However, the negative implication for income drawdown from deferred pension funds is possibly greatest. The government actuary figures (Appendix 1) may well have to be adjusted to take into account income falls of up to 20% and those taking drawdown may have to pull in their belts or radically increase the value of their pension funds.

This is a time of great change in retirement planning and invest-ment planning and the need for adequate advice to plan properly has never been greater. Not to plan effectively could cost you dearly – at both the funding stage and the actual retirement stage.

Coupled with this is the rising cost of retirement. At present, a couple on national average earnings planning to retire at age 65 with the target of two-thirds retirement income will require a capital sum of at least £100,000 to purchase a pension of £6,000 at current annuity rates, with an escalating income.

The average UK house price in March 1997 was £54,000. Many people look upon their home as their longest and largest savings commitment and their greatest asset when the house is paid off. However, to meet their target retirement income, they will need a pension fund of *double* the average value of a house in the UK.

Moreover, improvements in life expectancy will make pensions more expensive to buy as annuity rates will be lower. A two-year improvement in life expectancy will increase the purchase price of a pension for a 65-year-old by 5%. If annuity rates are falling, then instead of the £100,000 capital required, the effect of falling annuity rates, lower mortality rates through people living longer and the increased cost of guarantees could increase the two-thirds target pension for the retiring couple to £120,000.

In the longer term, people will either have to contribute more to pension funding or make sure that their pension fund returns are higher not lower than expected. Making the correct investment and retirement decisions will be even more crucial in the future. However, without knowing what the various options are, or without an understanding of the financial mechanics of the retirement process, this would be a most difficult task for most people.

The *choices* to be made will be *different* for everyone, depending on their circumstances and no one choice stands head and shoulders above any other – apart from the need to preserve capital whilst increasing income, and to have a workable investment strategy.

Key points summary

This chapter covered the following crucial areas:

- Decisions at *retirement date* for best income and capital preservation options.
- The employed with occupational schemes as well as the self-employed with personal pensions and retirement annuities and others.
- The full range of options at retirement, including best income choices and best safety and guarantee options.
- The different retirement products, including full descriptions of annuities.
- Comparisons between the various choices of conventional annuity, income drawdown or phased retirement.

Action plan

1. Complete the options at retirement list on page 94.   ❑
2. Select best income choices or safety and guarantee options. ❑
3. Decide on your overall retirement strategy. Are you most suited towards conventional annuities ❑; income drawdown ❑; phased retirement ❑; or a combination of the above ❑?
4. How much income do you need? £_____ From when? _____ For how long? _____ Can you supplement your income? _____
5. Can you accept investment risk? _____ If so, how much, for your growing pension fund, or the annuity which you must take? _____
6. If you are at the retirement contemplation stage and it's looking complex, consult an independent financial adviser to assist you with your options. ❑

CHAPTER 7

Investment Planning Strategies For Retirement

When I was young I thought money was the most important thing in life; now that I am old I know it is.
Oscar Wilde

Objective: **To effectively plan your investment strategies throughout the retirement process to ensure that you obtain maximum investment performance for capital growth, as well as income, depending on your risk profile and your circumstances at the time**

Making the right investment decisions at the right time can literally increase your investment portfolio by thousands of pounds, whereas making the wrong investment decisions at the wrong time could prove to be financially disastrous.

The retirement investment planning process covers many different periods, depending on your circumstances, your station in life, and what you want your money to do for you. That is why following the strategies outlined in this chapter could not only save you thousands of pounds, but could significantly increase your investment portfolio, leading to a financially-secure retirement.

THE INVESTMENT PROCESS

Strategy	Period
Retirement fund and investment accumulation	Working life
⇓	⇓
Retirement countdown with accelerated accumulation of funds	10 years before retirement
⇓	⇓
Investment options from lump sum	At retirement
⇓	⇓
Retirement income and investment management	In retirement
⇓	⇓
Reinvestment for income and capital growth	For dependants and heirs

Your investment planning strategies will not only encompass investment savings and putting more into pension funds, but should also look at the debt liability side of your personal balance sheet: would it be more appropriate to pay off your mortgage earlier, to reduce your outgoings through paying off expensive credit cards, to retain more profits in your business in order to increase your shareholder values, or merely to plan on how to use the business assets as your own when you go off into retirement. It is also not simply a matter of selecting the best tax-free investments available. Careful study may be required in relation to tax efficiency; the effect of charges on investment products reducing their overall performance as investments; how to use family members in your investment planning process (to build wealth through the use of their personal allowances and capital gains tax exemptions), and the creation of the best investment environment in relation to your personal circumstances.

For some people, it is merely a matter of putting away a certain sum of money into a growth investment each month and forgetting about it. For others it is a more conscious scientific process involving careful study of daily stock prices and the obtaining of information from many different sources. Investing, of course, takes on many different forms. Those with no faith in the ability of a world economy to return significant investment performance may well be persuaded to purchase gold coins or hard assets such as antiques, fine wines, art collections, classic cars, or whatever they fancy. These usually not only hold their value but significantly increase in value over the years, are easily passed from one generation to another, and are certainly not to be overlooked in the overall investment process.

Yet others may only consider investing in fixed assets such as commercial or residential properties with rental interest providing income and with steady capital growth underlying their property investment portfolios.

For most people, however, investment will take form of putting their hard-earned cash into a growth medium which will deliver significant performance over the years and will boost their pension and other income.

STRATEGY 75
Decide on what your risk profile is *before* investing – cautious, balanced or speculative

---

In short, no two investors are alike, each having preferred investment tastes over the other. However, they should both be looking for balance in their portfolios, consistent with their investment risk. For example, a balanced investor might have, say, 30% of his investments in building society and fixed interest investments, and 40-50% of his investments in either protected growth or equity-based products such as unit trusts, investment trusts, personal equity plans, endowment policies and so on. For his remaining 20-30%, he would be more speculative, possibly accepting a higher degree of risk in investing in equities, venture capital trusts, enterprise zone developments and so on.

The more cautious investor would have a far higher degree of assets, say 60-70%, in fixed interest or cash-backed investment, which would include TESSAs, National Savings, PIBS, and only, say, up to 30% in lower risk growth investments such as with-profit bonds, traded endowment with-profit policies and protected growth investment. (A protected growth investment is where the investor gets a proportion of the upside growth of the investment but is protected from the downward swings if they occur in the investment cycle.)

The higher the degree of risk which the investor is prepared to take on, the higher the level of more speculative-type investments which will be invested in. For example, if you have 40 years to go to retirement, you have a lot longer time for your investment either to perform, or to be changed for one that does and you could choose to be fully invested into equities, unit trusts, investment trusts, OEICS, investment bonds, enterprise investment schemes, venture capital trusts and others. More speculative investors with smaller amounts to invest may merely be content investing in a personal equity plan each year, up to the maximum amount allowed, whereas others will significantly build their own private share portfolios.

INVESTMENT RISK PROFILE

Type	Strategy	Period
Equity based	Growth funds can be higher risk	Working life
⇓		⇓
Within funds switch from unit-linked to with-profits or protected	Stable funds maintaining value-safety	2 years before retirement
⇓		⇓
Leave risk investments with income potential or maintain growth if income sufficient	Income-producing or more balanced growth depending on risk or requirements	At retirement
⇓		⇓

Type	Strategy	Period
Maintain portfolios or shift to higher income alternatives. Inheritance tax/safe investments, if possible	Maintain capital value and grow capital. Investments must produce income. Approach to investment risk is more cautious if capital base is small	In retirement
⇓		⇓
Higher equity growth investments or income producing	Depending on risk profile from ultra cautious to higher growth. Income possibly if required	For dependants

There is no doubt about it – our society has become a nation of investors. This has largely been driven by a succession of privatisation issues, where windfall profits have been made, following the sell-off of the UK's utilities (the nation's silverware) as well as by investing in share issues following the demutualisation of insurance companies and building societies.

STRATEGY 76
Follow commonsense investment principles. If it doesn't feel right, don't do it

---

Whatever your investment preferences, it is important to bear in mind the following investment principles:

- Only take on as much investment risk as you feel comfortable with. There is no point in making an investment and then worrying about it for the rest of your life.
- Make sure that your investment portfolio is properly balanced, depending upon your circumstances and risk preferences.
- Don't go for long-term investments whilst thinking short-term.

Long-term investments in equities, for example, are bound to have cyclical fluctuations where the investment values will go up and down. Too many people invest for the long term, but then worry unnecessarily about short-term fluctuations.

- Always invest to be ahead in real terms. Inflation will be with us forever – and investments which do not outperform inflation are actually losing you money in real terms.
- Choose your fund managers carefully, as some are more successful than others on a consistent basis.
- Avoid high-charging products; opt for performance-related fees if possible.
- Be prepared to adapt to change. If your investment risk profile alters due to changes in your circumstances, then don't be afraid to move or to cut your losses.
- Don't be panicked into making hasty investment decisions which may cost you dearly in the future. For example, should your investment performance in an investment fall over a period, then remember you haven't lost anything unless you sell. Within a year of Black Monday, when investment values across the board fell by 30% or more, most investors in the equity markets were back where they started.
- If you have a preference for fixed interest investments such as gilts, remember that these are market-sensitive to interest rate changes. A rise in interest rates could mean a reduction of your capital invested, whereas a fall in interest rates could increase your capital invested.
- Above all, go for an investment risk spread. Don't have all your eggs in one basket, not even within the same investment type or group.
- Wherever possible, make sure that you are utilising all your available tax allowances and exemptions, consistent with your investment risk profile.
- Know that there are risks in an investment where it is difficult to realise that investment should you require the cash. In recent years some people fell into the property investment trap, ended up with negative equity, couldn't find tenants for their properties, and their investment turned into a liability nightmare.
- If something is successful, then you have nothing to lose by following it.
- Be prepared to fine-tune your investment portfolio from time to time, keeping it current with your objectives and your performance criteria.

- Don't be selfish with your investments. Consider investing for your spouse and children, and grandchildren, if they are important to you and if you have sufficient disposable capital and income beyond your own need requirements.
- Watch out for 'get rich quick' tips. By the time you get the tip, it may well be too late and all you are doing is fuelling someone else's 'get rich quick' scheme.
- Begin your investment programme as soon as possible, even if the amounts which you start off with are small. The greatest compounding effect actually occurs towards the end of your investment's life, and the sooner you start, the better. Delaying your investment decision by one year over a 20-year period, could cost you up to 20% or more in value of your eventual end fund.
- Prioritise your investment allocation to fit your investment profile. Most people have scarce resources of capital for investment purposes and will need to allocate precise capital amounts consistent with their need requirements and their short, medium and long-term objectives. For example, whilst your long-term objective in retirement may well be to produce income from your capital, it would, in all likelihood, be the wrong strategy for you to invest merely for income 20 or 30 years before, without giving any consideration to capital growth.
- Remember that investing is fun, and a number of investors prefer to handle at least part of their own investment portfolio (whether they do badly with it or not) rather than entrust it to investment managers or advisers. There is nothing wrong with this approach and, in fact, it is to be encouraged because you maintain an interest in investment matters and develop an expertise as an investor which you may not ordinarily have had. Whole acres of rain forest have gone into producing books on investments to help you, and if you are just starting out, you should read the *Investors Chronicle Beginner's Guide to Investment* published by Century Business.

STRATEGY 77
Learn about investments so that you can clearly communicate what you want to invest in

---

Before moving on to strategies which will significantly build your wealth, it is important to emphasise that clarity of communication between investors and their advisers is essential. According to the Securities and Investment Board, the biggest cause for complaint from investors was that they were put into the wrong type of investments for their investment risk profile by investment advisers. Unless it was a case of self-interest on the part of your financial adviser, the only reason why you would be in a different type of investment to the one you thought you were in, is because there has been a breakdown of communication and exchange of information. If you consider the investment risk spectrum line below, at the left hand end of the line are the most conservative or cautious investments, whereas, at the extreme right of the line are the most speculative investments.

Most cautious	Balanced	Most speculative
TESSAs	Endowments, unit trusts, investment trusts, with-profit bonds, PEPs	Equities, VCTs, EISs, unquoted companies
Building society, national savings, fixed interest investments		
Low or nil growth		Highest growth possible

The above risk investment profile line obviously does not include every single investment available, but will give you an idea of the underlying risky nature of investments. Those more given towards producing income, but without capital growth, are towards the most cautious end of the investment spectrum, whereas those which are designed to deliver higher levels of capital growth are towards the more speculative end.

Ninety-nine per cent of investors have only a very narrow perception of the different types of investments and their risk profiles. There has never been a full study which has risk-rated every single investment product available, so, if your knowledge is limited, you will make decisions based on that limited knowledge. The knowledge of your financial adviser should be much wider and could offer you more scope, but only if communication between you is clear.

The following scenario is quite common. The investor may speak to his financial adviser, who asks him whether is a cautious, balanced or speculative investor. The client, not knowing the terms of reference, indicates he is a *balanced* investor. The financial adviser then places the client into a balanced investment portfolio which, in his opinion, would contain personal equity plans, with-profit bonds, and possibly an endowment policy. However, 'balance' in the mind of the client means he would like 50% of investments in fixed deposits in a building society, with the other half going into National Savings. His conception of 'balanced' is totally different from that of the financial adviser. It is therefore important that if you are going to become your own financial expert, you understand the make-up of investments in order to get the correct investment spread for yourself. The investor in the above example was, in fact, a 'most cautious' investor who had really only considered fixed interest non-capital growth investments for his portfolio.

Some of the investment strategies given below will overlap with others, depending on your actual position in the retirement planning process at any one time. A number of strategies will be generic to all aspects of the investment process, whereas others will be more specific to an actual event or period in your lifetime. It is essential that you develop your own strategic investment plan and, to this end, you may wish to draw strategies applicable to yourself from the various sections.

INVESTING DURING YOUR WORKING LIFE

Your overall investment strategy will be to consider maximum funding into pension schemes, whether self-employed or employed, and then making up the balance of any investment requirements to supplement your pension in retirement. Earlier chapters dealt with these aspects and you may wish to refresh yourself on your funding objectives by looking at Chapter 3 again.

Your working life is the build-up period. Family commitments, and possibly business liabilities, may mean that there is not that much disposable income over for alternative investments or, indeed, pension funding itself, but towards the latter stages of your working life more disposable income should become available to be used for either pension boosters or appropriate investment planning.

STRATEGY 78
**Choose the appropriate pension scheme for your
needs and get the investment funding properly
allocated**

If you are employed and on your employer's occupational
pension scheme, you may make additional pension contributions
to either the AVC part of your employer's scheme, or, better still,
into a free standing additional voluntary contribution scheme.
You have no control at all over the AVC component of your
employer's scheme, even though you may well be contributing
towards it. Your employer will be setting the investment strategy
for this scheme, more than likely without consulting you.
However, if you have elected to take an FSAVC, then the ball is
entirely in your court. You can decide into what sort of
investment your AVC will go, and, indeed, which product
provider to choose, which will offer you the investment spread
that you require.

Whilst past performance is, indeed, no guarantee of future
performance, you can get a little help along the way. Some
pension product providers do offer these arrangements at a
discount (meaning less charges on the scheme) or, to entice you
into the product, will offer an additional bonus allocation or an
allocation of value. Some product providers may offer an
additional free 3-6 months' contributions – others will merely
offer an uplift in percentage terms. In one case, I managed to
obtain in excess of 16% additional allocation from a particular
company for a single premium personal pension plan. Naturally,
the client was most delighted with this, as it actually guaranteed
his first year investment performance of at least 16%! Some
companies may have a higher charging structure, but have consistently delivered on performance, so ultimately it becomes a
matter of choice.

You may wish to choose a scheme where you can make
switches on a regular basis, should you require this, between one
fund and another. If this is your intention – to actively manage
your pension investment portfolio – then you would probably be
better off with a fund which does not charge for making switches
between different types of internal investments.

The same principle applies if you are self-employed, or a

partner, or eligible for a personal pension plan. There are two different types of personal pension plan available. The first is where the insurer or pensions provider makes the investment management decision for you – and your instructions to the fund manager on how he should be managing the funds will fall on deaf ears. The second, if you consider yourself an expert in these matters and are looking for a lower charging structure product, is where you can make your own investment decisions in a self-invested personal pension plan (a SIPP). Your financial adviser can set one of these up for you for a fee, and also advise you on which investments to make. *You* have a choice, which includes investing in other insurance companies' top performing funds. Winterthur, for example, not only encourages this choice, but also has a most flexible charging structure and has been the market leader in SIPP provision for a number of years.

STRATEGY 79
If self-employed, or a partner, or employed but with no pension scheme, choose a SIPP or a competent fund manager with a good track record

---

If you wish to direct your personal investment strategy with regard to how your pension funds are invested, then make use of a self-invested personal pension plan as described above. However, if you feel that choosing investments and managing them is not within your field of expertise, then make sure you choose a product provider with a competent fund manager who has delivered on past performance. Even though past performance is no indication of future performance, it certainly goes a long way to satisfying you that a particular fund manager has done it once and is possibly more likely to do it again. Be prepared to make meaningful contributions, though. Different providers will have varying limits for minimum contributions – unless, of course, you are transferring funds from other schemes to a SIPP to make use of its greater flexibility.

Unlike a free standing additional voluntary contribution scheme, where you can only have one FSAVC from one product provider in any one year, you can spread your investment risk amongst as many personal pension plan providers as you like. It is the aggregate allowances which count and, at the end of the day, all of your schemes are brought into account for that aspect.

STRATEGY 80
Review your pension investments regularly

This applies equally to those who manage, or are responsible for, money purchase schemes, investments underpinning final salary schemes, group personal pension arrangements and so on. You need to review constantly not only the scheme rules (especially since the Pensions Act 1995 became effective in April 1997) but also the investment philosophy and strategies underpinning larger pension funds. The same thing goes for sponsors of SSAS schemes, who must ensure that there is sufficient liquidity within the SSAS scheme to enable members to retire. For example, some SSAS schemes have invested in commercial properties, which may have to be sold in order to provide sufficient retirement income for retiring members.

STRATEGY 81
Decide whether to be your own investment expert or to seek appropriate investment advice

Professional or experienced investors may well decide to research the investment market themselves and make their own decisions in respect of their pension funding. Less sophisticated investors will be better off by not only seeking professional investment advice, but ensuring that their investment funds within their pension schemes are actively monitored and managed. Squeezing that extra 1 or 2%, or maybe even 10%, performance out of your pension fund assets will certainly go a long way towards boosting your eventual funds.

STRATEGY 82
Choose a consistent fund manager with a good track record of performance

If a fund is performing poorly, then part of the fault could lie with you and your investment strategy. This is certainly the case with larger pension schemes which may have the most conservative asset allocation, seen as a protection measure against falling capital values. The fund manager then doesn't have much scope to exceed his investment brief, as he or she is operating under instructions from the client to invest in certain areas only. By giving your fund manager far greater discretion, the make-up of the pension fund and whether it is merely at a growth stage, or whether the fund itself has matured so that it can begin paying out pensions, will determine the investment allocation mix for the fund. The following table illustrates what the pooled investment performance has been in various sectors over the last few years. It sets out the median returns achieved by the UK Pooled Pension Funds participating in the CAPS survey over cumulative periods ending 31 March 1996.

Annualised returns	1yr %	2yrs %	3yrs %	4yrs %	5yrs %	6yrs %	7yrs %	8yrs %	9yrs %	10yrs %
UK Equities (All Active)	25.9	12.7	14.1	16.9	13.6	12.6	11.8	13.2	10.9	13.0
UK Smaller Cos	32.9	12.3	15.9	17.4	13.9	10.0	6.8	8.7	7.7	11.4
UK Equities (Standard)	24.9	12.9	13.7	16.4	13.5	13.1	12.4	13.6	11.2	13.1
Overseas	26.9	9.5	14.5	17.5	14.1	10.7	10.8	12.2	8.5	10.5
Global Equity	26.6	11.4	13.9	17.3	14.2	13.1	-	-	-	-
North America	**40.4**	**19.2**	14.1	18.5	17.6	15.9	15.8	15.7	11.0	10.5
Europe	29.5	12.9	17.1	17.1	15.2	9.2	13.1	14.7	9.7	9.7
Japan	12.2	-0.6	8.4	14.8	7.5	6.1	1.7	4.1	4.9	9.2
Far East[1]	29.5	10.6	**21.2**	**24.4**	**22.0**	**17.8**	**19.7**	**20.7**	**16.6**	**21.7**
Far East[2]	18.8	2.4	14.5	18.4	12.6	9.7	9.6	-	-	-
Emerging Markets	24.5	-11.6	-	-	-	-	-	-	-	-
UK Bonds	10.4	6.2	7.2	11.0	11.2	13.1	10.8	10.1	10.1	9.9
International Bonds	14.2	7.2	6.6	13.7	13.9	-	-	-	-	-
Index-Linked	7.6	4.2	4.9	9.5	8.1	8.7	7.9	9.0	7.9	8.8
Cash	6.4	5.9	5.8	6.6	7.5	8.8	9.7	9.8	9.8	9.9
Property	3.6	4.6	10.2	7.4	6.3	3.9	4.6	7.5	8.9	8.8
Mixed with property	22.6	10.5	12.6	15.4	13.0	12.3	11.5	12.5	10.6	11.5
Non-property Mixed	23.3	11.6	12.9	15.7	13.3	12.6	12.3	12.9	10.4	11.5

Notes: [1]Excluding Japan equities [2]Including Japan

The best performing sector over each period is highlighted in **bold** typeface

Source: Bacon and Woodrow, *Pension Pocket Book 1997*

The trend may well be away from top performance towards more protectionism as a result of the increased duties placed on fund trustees under the new Pension Act 1995 which became effective in April 1997. There is therefore a danger that this trend could result in reduced investment performances in the longer term.

STRATEGY 83
Decide on an investment strategy and stick to it

Probably one of the most successful investment managers in the world is Warren Buffet, whose success has been in choosing blue chip stocks and staying with the same ones for periods up to and in excess of 25 years. He requires and expects investment performance in the very long term.

That's Warren's strategy. The investment strategy of someone like George Soros (who cornered the market in currency exchange rates at one time) is to choose the precise moment to enter the market, take a profit, and then leave the market. The actions of this one man can actually be responsible for fixing the foreign exchange interest rates on currencies for all countries across the globe. Yet, where there are winners, there are also going to be losers with that type of strategy.

Some fund managers may have an entirely different approach. Instead of following market trends investing in, say, a basket of blue chip equities in the various world stock exchanges, they will specifically research and stock-pick a company which has shown consistent profitability over a number of years, has a good track record, has sound management in place and where the share value is calculated to be more than the price of the share on the Stock Exchange. The stock pickers will, therefore, only buy shares with embedded values in them, and will stick to that process. Using this method, at least one group has consistently returned over 40% per annum over the last five years.

Your choice of fund manager, and therefore product provider, is most important, to deliver consistent upper quartile investment returns on your portfolio. It is therefore vital to choose a fund manager with a similar investment ethos to yours. For example, one fund manager will consistently only purchase poorly-performing stocks (where the cost of purchase is cheap) feeling that, through the investment cycle over, possibly, a five-year period, for example, these choices will outperform the average offered by the Stock Exchange.

STRATEGY 84
Choose consistently high performers for your investments

This point cannot be emphasised too much. A consistently high investment performer in a product with a lower charging structure will not only save you thousands of pounds in the long term, but will also take a lot of the financial strain which many people experience in respect of funding. Let me explain it in this way.

If your hard-earned money is not sweating for you once invested then, in order to meet your financial objectives in retirement, you will need to make more of a contribution and this will diminish your capital or income resources for other requirements or projects. By enabling the fund to take the investment strain, where you may not have been able to afford maximum pension contribution funding in the past, some of your investment shortfall will possibly be made up through added-value and enhanced performance. I'm sure you get the picture.

STRATEGY 85
Choose growth investments during your working life

Although the building societies would like to say differently, the only thing that can be guaranteed when investing in a building society is that your investment will not grow or even keep pace with inflation over the longer term. Building society investments are generally perceived as safer investments. However, if you are out to build a growth fund, and you have plenty of investment years ahead of you, you need to be more adventurous in your approach and should consider growth investments. (That is not to say that you cannot have growth investments with some protection.) The following table shows you how equities have outperformed building society investments over a given period.

EQUITIES V. BUILDING SOCIETY SHARES

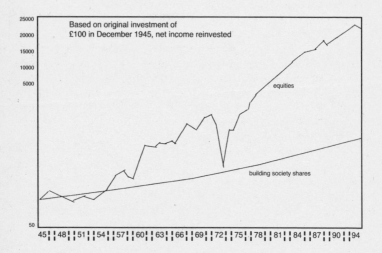

Source: Barclays de Zoete Wedd Securities Limited

STRATEGY 86
Make pension funding your flagship investment vehicle

Your best long-term investment will be in your pension fund. Not only are the contributions tax deductible to you (the Inland Revenue pays a proportion of your contributions in this way), but at present the investment growth in the fund is untaxed and your investment will grow through to maturity at a higher level than other investments where the dividends and interest element are taxed. One of the next best investment strategies for individuals is to maximise their personal equity plans. In the 1997/98 tax year you may invest a total of £9,000 into a personal equity plan, of which £6,000 per person can go into a general PEP and £3,000 can go into a specific single company PEP. These investments all accept regular contributions as well as single premium contributions.

The same can be said for investments into unit trusts, investment trusts and OEICS. These three investments enable a pooling, as well as pound cost averaging investment strategy to be undertaken as well as a diversification of your portfolio. There are literally thousands of unit trusts and other funds available, both in the UK and offshore, enabling a wide variety of choices to be made. If you have lump-sum investments to be made, consider investing in a with-profits bond where the bonuses accruing to your investment are smoothed and where minimum guarantees are offered through the product provider in respect of bonus allocations. Other investment bonds are insurance-based and offer additional flexibility in respect of inheritance tax planning, as well as income drawdown in later years.

A thriving investment market has been built up over the last few years in respect of traded endowment with-profit policies, and for those with a slightly higher level of risk, there are plans available whereby these traded endowment with-profit policies can be bought in and geared through loans to provide you with even more traded endowments as an investment.

Other investment plans which have provided a consistent base for regular savings over the years have been endowment policies which have been more commonly associated with school fees planning and mortgage redemption schemes. To a certain extent these have fallen out of favour due to their high charging structures, but still remain a part of many people's investment portfolios.

STRATEGY 87
Fund for growth investments during your working life

Whatever the investment (and I have not covered all of them here), the main point is that, during your working life, you need to be funding for growth investments and the younger you are, the fewer guarantees you will require to safeguard your capital.

More cautious investors may require the benefits of growth, as well as the benefits of protection of capital. To this end, there are a number of protected growth investments available, which usually track the FT-SE or some other index. The principle underlying this kind of investment is that you receive a proportion of the growth earned by your money (usually not the full amount, but between 70 and 95% is the average of any investment growth during any particular quarter), but will not experience any of the downside should there not be any investment performance during any one calendar quarter. In other words, your capital is protected and, depending upon the amount of risk you are willing to undertake, you will receive varying elements of capital growth.

With the wide diversity of different investment products and schemes available, it is usually in your interests to take professional advice to ensure that you are investing in plans not only consistent with your investment risk profile, but also with your long-term retirement objectives. Remember that investing your pension fund will, over 40 years, bring you a pension of a maximum two-thirds of your final salary if in an occupational pension scheme – more if in certain other schemes. The balance you will have to make up through additional investment funding.

This initial investment growth accumulation phase takes place during the whole of your working life and is significantly boosted when you get to within 10 years of retirement.

TEN YEARS BEFORE RETIREMENT

The retirement countdown planning period is usually 10 years before normal retirement date, but can be as short as 2-5 years.

This is the period of readiness for retirement. From your retirement countdown chart which you prepared earlier (see Chapter 1), you will know which commitments have to be met and when. This is also the period when some investments – such as endowment policies – will begin to mature and will require reinvestment in order to boost eventual retirement capital and income.

STRATEGY 88
Maximise investment funding and decide whether or not to defer your retirement date

---

From an investment planning point of view, the retirement countdown period is divided into two parts. The first is a growth spurt phase, usually for investments other than retirement funds, whereas the second part occurs between one and two years before actual retirement date, when more volatile equity investments should be placed into protected growth funds so as not to lose vital capital value at this essential stage. This is particularly the case should you decide that you will be taking your annuity from actual retirement date and not extending or deferring your retirement date until the maximum age of 75. This is the position where you are either self-employed, or a partner, or a member of a retirement annuity or personal pension plan.

If, however, you are employed and a member of an occupational pension scheme, then the value of your pension and your lump sum will be determined by your years of service and your final remuneration, with the protection of your retirement capital not entering into the picture.

For both the employed and the self-employed, the retirement countdown process is the period where you will want to maximise your investment funding, as well as your pension contributions. You may wish to put yourself on to an accelerated fast-track in respect of funding investments, as well as pension funds, and you will begin making plans during this period for the redemption of any outstanding liabilities which may occur at retirement such as outstanding mortgages, credit card debts, hire purchase agreements and other liabilities such as loans.

It may pay you to redeem the capital element of your mortgage some years early, thereby saving thousands of pounds' worth of interest. This could well prove to be a better investment for some people than merely investing in fixed interest or equity based investments.

STRATEGY 89
Pay off your mortgage and other liabilities early, as part of your investment programme

---

Early capital redemption on mortgages, if you have not done so already, will provide you with great peace of mind and release from financial stress in that your house will be paid off before your retire. Naturally, this process can be begun much earlier than waiting until the retirement countdown phase of your investment programme, and by reducing your mortgage liability, you will save thousands of pounds of interest in the long run. It may also generate extra capital in that you may be left with an endowment or other repayment vehicle to be diverted to your retirement programme.

STRATEGY 90
Accelerate your investment programme by making booster investments at this time

---

If you are 10 years from retirement, you will more than likely have finished bringing up your family. You can now concentrate on your retirement planning and focus in on this major objective. It is crucial that you do everything possible to boost your retirement funding.

Single premium contributions can be made towards pension funding if you are self-employed or have previously generated unused tax reliefs through applying the carry back/carry forward provisions to get your lump sum pension contributions tax relievable (see Strategy 29). If you are employed, you will want to maximise your contributions to AVCs or FSAVCs. Remember, under current legislation, you may contribute up to 15% of your final remuneration, including the value of your benefits-in-kind such as your company car, in order to boost your pension contributions. Regular savings plans should also be increased if at all possible, and maximum use should be made of tax-exempt investments using other people's money to boost your investment funds. In this case, other people's money (OPM) belongs to the Inland Revenue, and you are quite within your rights to allow the Inland Revenue to assist you with your investment building if the investment qualifies for this kind of tax relief. Typical investments for those able to afford them would include venture capital trusts, where currently each individual may invest up to £100,000 and have up to 20% of the investment value as a deduction from their actual tax liability in any one tax year.

STRATEGY 91
If a higher rate taxpayer make maximum use of tax exemptions, personal allowances and tax-efficient products

---

Apart from pension funding, and venture capital trusts mentioned above, there are a number of other tax-efficient investment areas which you may wish to consider. Investors who have spare capital and a higher preference for risk, may decide to invest into unquoted high-growth companies. Under the Enterprise Investment Scheme initiative, if the company qualifies for EIS relief, you may invest up to £100,000 per person in each tax year into such unquoted investee companies, and obtain a reduction in your actual tax liability of 20% of the investment made.

Tax planning is also important here, and you may use this device to back-date a part of your tax relief into the previous tax year. If you prefer a lower risk investment, you may well be tempted to invest into an Enterprise Zone investment or an Enterprise Zone Trust. Up to 100% of your investment will reduce your taxable income and may even bring you into a lower tax bracket. Rents from commercial properties are presently producing between 7 and 9% gross. Most Enterprise Zone development investments can also be geared through using loans, where the loan interest is offsettable against your rental income. You should also expect reasonable growth in the investment properties and a number of Enterprise Zone developments now offer guaranteed income, even if the properties are unlet.

While EZT investments are generally for a period of at least seven years, investments into venture capital trusts and enterprise investment scheme investments must be for five years in order for you to benefit from tax relief. Enterprise Zone investments are subject to capital gains tax when you sell them; however, there are reliefs available which should be considered during your planning process.

Again, depending upon your risk profile, you may wish to invest instead in investments which provide you with tax-free income or tax-free capital growth. These would include personal equity plans, and venture capital trust investments.

STRATEGY 92
Save further tax through providing investments for your spouse or partner

---

Every individual person, irrespective of age, can be a taxpayer and has personal allowances, which means that a certain part of any taxable income can accrue in their hands tax free. Consider this aspect as part of your investment and tax planning.

STRATEGY 93
Begin making preparations to exit your business
successfully

The last 10 years before retirement is when the business owner should begin thinking about how best to exit the business, whether by selling it, liquidating it, providing for management to take it over, or whatever route it applicable to his or her particular circumstances. Many, in fact, get to retirement age, having done nothing about this aspect, and with no prior planning.

Usually if you sell the business assets, or a share in a business, the proceeds are subject to capital gains tax in your hand. At retirement age (from age 50, so long as you have had the business for at least 10 years) there are generous retirement reliefs which will reduce the incidence of any capital gains tax payable on your hard-earned capital. The first £250,000 worth of your business assets is free of capital gains tax and the next £750,000 worth of your business assets is free of CGT up to 50%. The balance is subject to capital gains tax at your highest rate of tax.

There are exit strategies which can be planned, which will save you capital gains tax on the whole amount, prior to selling your assets – otherwise you are forced into a situation where you must reinvest your capital gain in order to defer any tax payable. At present, there is only one route for reinvesting a capital gain in order to obtain deferment relief, and that is through investing into a qualifying Enterprise Investment Scheme unquoted company.

However, in my experience, the last thing most people want to do is invest up to 50% of their hard-earned wealth from their businesses into someone else's business, where they may have little or no control. This is definitely an area where you require expert advice, which may include merely paying the capital gains tax and reinvesting the balance of your capital received into an investment of your choice.

Some astute business owners, knowing that it would be difficult to sell the business to an outsider, should possibly begin setting up an employee share owner trust to enable the management and employees to purchase the business at the appropriate time.

STRATEGY 94
If your business is your pension, make sure business capital is wisely invested

---

Many business owners have poor pension provision because they have retained the business profits within the business in order to have stronger balance sheets. If this is the case, and you do not require the business capital for expansion or development purposes, then make sure that the business invests its money wisely. This can be into protected growth investments, or into high-yielding interest accounts.

For those who still require retained reserves as working capital within the business, look at bringing these retained reserves out of the business as a dividend, significantly reducing the rate of tax payable on these reserves. Money thus removed from the business can either come back into the business by way of a loan account, or it can be invested efficiently – possibly offshore.

From an inheritance tax planning point of view, remember that a director's loan account is an asset in your estate, and could be subject to inheritance taxes. However, the value of any shares may qualify for business property relief on your death and be 100% exempt from your estate. It is therefore preferable, if you are planning to increase the build-up of your personal wealth outside the business, as well as outside your estate, to consider inheritance tax-efficient growth investments such as a director's loan account redemption scheme.

STRATEGY 95
If possible, get your money out of the company and invest it in a growth medium in your own hands

---

There are plenty of live examples where personal funds are grossly mismanaged through being left in the business. This usually happens in the case of director's loan accounts, where the director has loaned money to the business, or where dividends have accumulated on behalf of a shareholder and are left in the business.

From the point of view of the business owner, leaving money in the business will strengthen the balance sheet, but remember that a director's loan account is actually a liability to the business, which must be repaid at some stage. It is not the same as retained reserves, where the business has already paid tax, and which is left to accumulate in a bank account or treasury account.

Take the example of Martin Powis, who provided loan capital, along with other shareholders, to a company over 10 years ago. Martin's £50,000 10 years ago is still only worth £50,000 (less, if we take inflation into account) today. It is unlikely that Martin is earning any interest, or perhaps at a very low rate, through lending his money to the business. Ten years ago there may well have been good reasons to have adopted this business financing strategy, but today general inertia has meant that Martin has not bothered to redeem his loan from the company.

Had he invested the £50,000 lump sum into a growth investment in his name, over a 10-year period it could well be worth over £200,000 now, and if the business required working capital, it could get that from a bank, using Martin's new investment as security if required. Any interest paid by the company on any bank borrowings used for commercial purposes is, of course, tax deductible to the business.

At the end of the day, Martin is going to retire, but the business is probably going to carry on. The strategy involved may require new financing arrangements for the business to enable Martin to build his personal wealth in order to boost his capital in retirement.

STRATEGY 96
If you are a partner in a partnership, plan now to get 100% of your capital account on retirement

---

Probably the most vulnerable business entity is the partnership. If there are not prior business or partnership agreements in place, on the death of a partner, his heirs and dependants have an immediate call for cash from the surviving partners for the full value of his share.

I recently came across a firm of accountants which had six partners. Three of those partners were nearing retirement age and three were in their mid-forties. If the three who were due to retire were to go off together, the financial strain of removing their capital accounts from the partnership (which required them as working capital) would have meant the collapse of the partnership. Even if they didn't take their full capital accounts out with them, the surviving three partners would still be under financial strain in having to make capital instalment payments to the retiring partners.

In fact, this is what usually happens. When a partner retires, his capital account is repaid to him, usually with nominal interest, over a period of up to 10 years. That may be fine for the partnership, but is generally not very satisfactory for the partner concerned. He wants his money, and he wants it now. It is therefore important that partnerships set in place proper capital account redemption schemes and provide the partnership agreement planning which is required.

Lack of adequate planning of this nature is endemic, especially amongst professional practices. It often leads to a spate of mergers following the retirement or departure of a partner and, in some instances, the loss of capital account capital which is rightly the after-tax profits of the individual partner concerned. This is a very complex area and it requires proper planning.

STRATEGY 97
If you have valuable share options, ensure proper tax planning

---

Exercising a share option has different tax consequences, depending on whether your scheme is approved or unapproved. If approved, then the exercise of the option gives rise to a capital gains tax liability, whereas if your scheme is unapproved, the granting and exercise of share options will be subject to income tax. Planning in this case could include, for example, the gifting of the share option to your spouse in order to utilise any personal allowances or lower tax bands, thus ensuring that you end up with a higher level of retained capital than had you to pay additional tax on it.

It may even be possible to forgo the share option and have it cancelled, on condition that the company provides a booster to your pension scheme or some other bonus diversion arrangement. Once you actually exercise the option, there is very little which can be done in respect of income tax mitigation. If you suffered a capital gain, after your annual exemption is taken into account, as

well as indexation on the gain, you can defer any tax payable
through investing into an unquoted qualifying investment.

STRATEGY 98
**If you have pension schemes with a number of
different employers, now is the time to
consolidate them**

If you have been a particularly mobile employee during your
working life, the chances are that you may well have built up
pension benefits with different employers, some of whom may not
even be in existence any more.

At least one firm of independent financial advisers provides a
useful tracking service, going back over your employment history,
and finding out about pension schemes which were in existence
but about which you have no current knowledge. At the time you
probably thought you'd leave your benefits where they were,
allowing them to accumulate to retirement. Bad strategy!

The members of a pension scheme about which the pension
scheme sponsor is not very much concerned are those who have
left the scheme prior to retirement. The value of their funds is,
generally speaking, left to languish and, if never claimed, will no
doubt be distributed amongst the surviving members of the
pension scheme. It may well pay you to transfer your pension
rights through what is known as a buy-out bond, where those
funds can be properly invested on your behalf.

This would entail various actuarial calculations being made,
and also determining whether there were protected rights or not
in connection with your various pension schemes. Some life
offices specialise in what are known as Section 32 Buy-out Bonds,
whereas others would advise you to transfer your previous
pension funds either to your new employer (possibly using their
value to buy you more years of deemed service if in an
occupational scheme), or to a personal pension scheme where
they can be properly invested and monitored.

Get your financial adviser to write to all your previous
employers to ascertain the position in respect of your previous
funds.

STRATEGY 99
Get the most from the state scheme

If you have not done so already, now is the time to ensure that you can qualify for the maximum amount of state benefits possible. It may even pay you to consider your options in respect of paying back National Insurance contributions, especially for those periods where you may have worked abroad, or have not been on full employment. Obtain Form NP 38 from the DSS in order to ascertain your position. The same applies to your spouse, who may significantly be able to increase his or her state pension through buying back additional benefits. At the same time, get your financial adviser to establish whether, if you are contracted out of the State Earnings Related Pension Scheme (SERPS), you should contract back into the scheme in order to boost your state benefits.

We hope that, by nurturing your investment garden, you will soon be in a position to reap a bountiful crop. Certainly, the strategies mentioned above, for those within the retirement countdown process, will enable you to boost your investments at a time when you will need them to supplement your income in retirement.

Those at the end of their working lifetimes will also probably be on higher rates of tax and will be investing with tax efficiency in mind, including aspects such as 'bed and breakfasting' capital gains (selling off part of your portfolio to produce a capital gain so as to use your annual exemption, and then immediately re-investing it) – thus getting the tax man to help you save for your retirement – and consolidating your investments whilst, at the same time, getting rid of as many liabilities as possible.

Naturally, this is an ideal to which everyone would aspire. However, the real world is not an ideal scenario, and many people will only apply one or two of the strategies mentioned above as best fits their circumstances.

For example, take the case of the individual having to fund for school fees as well as providing retirement boosters. His priority will be to fund for the school fees, as they are of more immediate concern, leaving retirement funding till later. By then, it is often too late. However, there are school fees funding programmes which are loan-based, where the repayment vehicle can be part of the tax-free lump sum from your pension scheme. If you did not have such a scheme in place, you would usually be paying for school fees out of after-tax income. With the scheme, you can draw on your loan account, whilst maintaining boosted pension contributions into your pension scheme. These are also tax deductible to you. Although you may not have a greater lump sum at retirement, you will certainly have a larger pension from your fund than you had previously thought possible. In addition, because of the tax-free nature of your lump sum and the tax deductibility of your pension contributions, the Inland Revenue will ultimately end up by funding your school fees. This is not a bad strategy!

INVESTMENT PLANNING AT ACTUAL RETIREMENT DATE

Congratulations! You've arrived. For most people, retiring brings with it an overwhelming sense of relief – the gold watch has been collected from a generous employer and you can now look forward to the longest holiday of your life.

Strategies at the actual time of retirement can differ vastly, depending on your financial circumstances and whether you are able to carry on in employment, albeit of a limited nature. They will also depend on those income and capital resources available to you and how much of your retirement fund you have calculated you will actually need on a year-by-year basis.

Over the last few years, the restrictive rules, which previously forced people to take their pension and lump sum at the normal retirement date, have been replaced with a much more flexible regime, certainly for the self-employed or those with personal pension schemes and money purchase arrangements, and possibly in the future for those in occupational schemes.

The bottom line is this: depending upon your circumstances, it may well be better to leave as much of your pension fund as possible to continue to grow tax-free for as long as possible. Whilst there are with-profits or unit-linked growth annuities available, the vast bulk of annuities which are taken out are either level or escalating and there is no investment growth within the annuity itself. However, there *is* growth within the pension fund, and if immediate income is not a requirement until much later, you can defer taking some of your benefits for as long as possible – but only up until age 75, when you must finally take an annuity. These options were fully discussed in Chapter 6, in relation to income drawdown or phased retirement planning, both aspects being totally dependent upon your circumstances now and what they are likely to be in the future.

At *actual retirement date,* you will be concerned with the following major functions:

- The investment of any tax-free lump sum which will accrue from your pension funds.
- The investment of other lump sums from maturing investments, such as endowment policies and investment bonds.
- Investment of any surplus income.
- Income requirements from pension schemes and whether to take this as an income drawdown option or whether to take this by way of phased withdrawals of tax-free cash and pension annuities.
- Which annuity options to take and how to use the open market option most effectively.
- Final reduction of liabilities.
- The consolidation of cash lump sums from other sources such as the sale of the business or the sale of assets or even inheritances received.

Each of these aspects will require different types of planning and investment strategies. The main overriding concern will be for sufficient income in retirement. If at all possible, you will want your income to increase as the years go on, to compete with the effects of inflation. It is also understandable that your investment risk profile may well change radically. This will depend on how much you have available for investment, and whether you can afford to be speculative on what will, for many people, be their only capital amounts without any further capital accruing for later investment.

It is not surprising, therefore, that the most speculative investors up to retirement date suddenly become the most cautious investors from the retirement date onwards. Investments which were previously in higher growth, but also higher risk areas, will now be reconsidered for lower-to-nil growth but for maximum capital preservation. This will have to be balanced with the need for the highest levels of income and many investors will be tempted into so-called guaranteed investments and other areas offering higher than average income returns.

Some may even be tempted to enter into more speculative

investment arrangements such as the previously heavily-marketed home income plans whereby your house is remortgaged at retirement to provide you with investment capital. This process has been a disaster for many investors who lost their homes when investment performance fell and interest rates rose, thus making it impossible to service their mortgage arrangements. Since then, however, the market has reacted with similar drawdown schemes, using the home, but on a much more conservative basis.

To sum up, investors at retirement date are looking for capital preservation, capital growth, highest income or pension returns, the minimisation of debt, and the best investment planning strategies and options to suit their own circumstances. Above all, they would probably be looking for flexibility and the ability to move from one investment medium to another, should any prove to be unsatisfactory. They will also want to maximise their State benefits in respect of the State pension arrangements, whilst ensuring that they do not fall into the age allowance trap.

Those with significant estates will be considering estate planning and inheritance tax avoidance measures, the reduction of capital gains tax and its mitigation, especially with the sale of assets including business assets on retirement, and the most appropriate investments. Others will be considering emigration and retiring abroad, becoming non-domiciled, or merely re-arranging the streaming of their income.

Those who are in failing health at retirement, or who consider that at least a part of their retirement years is going to be spent in a residential or frail care facility, need to consider making the appropriate arrangements to prepare for that eventuality (see Chapter 10).

So, there are a number of investment strategies which need to be considered at the *actual date of retirement*, and the main ones are given here.

STRATEGY 100
At retirement, always take your tax-free lump sum

Both occupational pension schemes and personal pension plans, retirement annuities and most pension schemes – apart from AVCs and free-standing AVCs – offer a tax-free lump sum at retirement. Whilst the AVC or FSAVC does not allow you to withdraw a tax-free lump sum, it does, in fact, add to the value of the main fund, which, on aggregate, would allow a larger lump sum to be drawn from that area. Also, it is now possible not to bring your AVC or FSAVC into account when you retire from your main scheme, and the taking of a pension from these funds can be deferred.

If you are *self-employed, or a partner, or a member of a personal pension plan or retirement annuity plan, or any money purchase arrangement*, you have a choice either to use your whole fund to provide you with a pension or to take out a tax-free cash lump sum from your pension fund and use what remains to purchase a lower level of pension. It will always be more advantageous to you to take the tax-free lump sum, even if you only intend to invest it for income. This is because a voluntary annuity purchased from your own resources has a non-taxable element to it (whereas a pension coming directly from the fund is fully taxable), and you should have more income available to you by using your lump sum in this way. If you do not need the additional income, then at least you have the flexibility of when and how to invest your lump sum in order to provide you with further capital growth, or increased income, or a mixture of both.

Many people set aside a portion of their tax-free lump sum in order to redeem liabilities so that they can enter into retirement completely debt-free.

Let's not forget the fun element of retirement either. That long-awaited holiday or world cruise will be beckoning and you will need resources for the nice things in life. After all, you've worked hard to get there and you might as well enjoy it now!

The *timing* of when to take your lump sum is important and if you are on a phased retirement programme, you may wish to defer the taking of your lump sum until such time as you need it. You don't have to take the whole amount at once, and can also phase the taking of your lump sums at different periods. You will have decided, as in the previous chapter, what sort of retirement programme you will actually be on, and you should have decided which of your flexible options you are going to exercise.

The same situation applies if you are *employed and a member of an occupational pension scheme*, as you will be eligible for a commuted lump sum, as well as a pension arising from your pension fund. You will not have the same level of flexibility as the self-employed or partners; however, you will have other retire-

ment income benefits such as pensions which escalate in retirement, usually at a minimum of about 5%. Against this 5%
escalation, you must view whether your invested tax-free lump
sum is going to return more than 5%. This will usually be the
case, as an annuity purchased from private capital could give you
anything from, say, 8 to 20% and above, as a guaranteed fixed
return. The older you are, the more you will receive.

In all instances then, your best strategy would be to take your
lump sum and either to invest it for additional income or for
capital growth. This has the added advantage that, should you die
within the early years of your retirement, at least a part of the fund
is separately invested from your pension fund and is available for
your heirs and dependants. This is an important consideration,
bearing in mind the fact that, in most instances, if you have taken
your pension, your fund will die with you, apart from where
arrangements have been made for your dependants also to receive
a pension from that same fund.

STRATEGY 101
Your best investment strategy may be to defer taking
your pension for as long as possible

If you can afford to do so, and don't require the income immediately, or can manage on less, then your best investment option
may be to defer taking your pension or to defer the maturity of
your pension scheme for as long as possible. For those in employment, this may not be possible because of the rules of your occupational pension scheme. However, if you have a personal
pension plan, an AVC or an FSAVC, this may be possible up to age
75, when you will be forced to take your retirement benefits.

However, up until that time, the growth in your pension scheme
may continue to compound and you would have the option of
either drawing income from your pension scheme if you require
it, or having a phased withdrawal of your retirement benefits
(which would include a proportion of your lump sum as well as
an annuity at that time). Alternatively, you may merely wish to
leave your pension fund to accumulate until such time as you
actually need to use it.

The importance of tax-free compound growth cannot be under-
estimated and more and more people are seeking to defer the

taking of their pension benefits for as long as possible. For those who were unable to contribute to their original pension funding to the fullest extent possible early on, this is an ideal opportunity to have their pension scheme grow without any further contributions. If you continue to earn net relevant earnings, you may make further contributions into pension funding which will help to boost your overall fund until such time as you wish to take it. Another advantage is that, should you die in the pre-retirement period, your estate will have a return of your fund with interest, something which is not possible once you take your full retirement benefits.

STRATEGY 102
Delaying your retirement date as long as possible will guarantee you increased income

---

Annuity rates are directly determinable upon your age at the date of retirement if taking the benefit by way of an annuity. If you were due to retire from your personal pension plan at age 60, but you deferred the taking of your benefits for a further 15 years to the maximum allowed which is age 75, you now have a shorter period of survival, and the annuity rate is adjusted upwards to take into account those additional 15 years.

This factor alone will greatly increase your income from your annuities at retirement. The longer you can hold off taking them, the better the chances of a higher level of income. However, there may be a disadvantage to this approach in the short term, depending on the performance of interest rates at the time.

If interest rates are historically high at the time you are thinking about making your decision, and you only wish to defer the taking of your annuity for, say, two or three years, you may well be better off taking the annuity at a period of rising annuity rates than waiting for the shorter period to pass in the expectation of higher annuity rates. If income is surplus to your requirements, it could always be reinvested into other types of investments.

This can be a highly complex area of investment decision-making and should not be undertaken lightly. One should examine the trend of annuities and how interest rates have performed up until the time you wish to take your annuity, before making your absolute decision. However, it is true to say that if you expect to take it in another 15 years' time, then with the general trend of annuities upwards, plus your increased age, this will almost certainly guarantee you a higher annuity.

STRATEGY 103
Decide on your income requirements for your
retirement and plan accordingly

It is most important that you receive your cash flow analysis for the future and determine exactly what income is required and when. Once you have done this, you can decide how that income is going to accrue to you. When you begin the process, it often becomes irreversible, especially when annuities are taken, as they cannot be changed in the future. Remember, you may only have flexibility up to age 75. Then you have to make retirement investment decisions which will be with you for the rest of your life as far as annuities are concerned, but naturally you will have more flexibility with the disposition of your lump sum.

Once you have decided what your income requirements are (remembering to allow for inflation) as well as taking into consideration the possible need for future lump sums for whatever purposes, you should get together with a financial planner to adjust your financial and investment plan in keeping with your present circumstances and future requirements.

It is essential that you plan properly, and you will find that the products and services required at actual retirement date can be listed as follows:

- Consolidation of pension and annuity funds.
- Decisions as to deferment or otherwise of pensions.
- The best selection of annuity rates in respect of the open market option and any other option available at that time.
- The best investment of your lump sums for income and growth.
- Tax mitigation procedures and tax savings.
- Debt consolidation and repayment.
- Replacement of assets and 'perks' previously given to you by your company or employer.
- A schedule of investments, policies and maturing lump sums which are appropriately dated.

• General retirement advice, consistent with your requirements.

For most people, funds are probably in short supply and
products become very expensive as your age increases – for
example, in the health and protection market. Some of these may
even be unobtainable, depending on the state of your health – you
may be uninsurable, or the general high cost of health and
protection at increasing ages may be too much for you.

Only when you have determined your requirements can you
decide how to meet them. This will then dictate your overall
investment strategy, taking into account your preference or
otherwise for higher risk investments.

Your investments will have to be aligned with your income
requirements as well as your level of taxation and the allowances
available to you. As you get older, you need to be aware of the age
allowance trap which could seriously diminish your income.
Increasing income can reduce allowances. The higher rates of
allowance are reduced by £1 for each £2 of excess income over
£15,600, until the basic allowance is reached.

Proper retirement advice taken at this stage could literally save
you thousands of pounds. I have come across many retirees who
have merely accepted the advice of the pension fund provider in
respect of taking annuities from that particular product provider
and then have been left to their own devices in respect of
investment of their tax-free lump sums. There is only one
pensions product provider whom I have ever come across who
regularly advises clients to move their funds to take advantage of
the open market option. Most people suffer from inertia in that
they do not know what is available to them and remain loyal to
the product provider where they built up their pension scheme.
This could be disastrous for them in the long run, because all they
are doing is providing a cheap source of funds to the product
provider who, in turn, gives them a lower pension.

STRATEGY 104
Always take the open market option on retirement

Once you are in a position to take an annuity (at whatever stage of
the retirement process you decide to take it), unless your existing

pensions product provider is offering you a better deal, in 99% of cases you will probably be better off by moving your pension fund to a specialist annuity provider which is offering a better rate. This process is known as the open market option and is freely available to all people who have plans which qualify for it. On average, the minimum increase in additional pension income which you can expect from adopting the open market option is about 11%. Some shifts for the open market option can produce 25% or more in increased income at that time, as was illustrated in the diagram in Strategy 67.

If you built up a *personal pension plan*, the maximum tax-free lump sum is 25%. This remains, should you utilise the open market option. However, if you built up your funds through a *retirement annuity*, the utilisation of the open market option will reduce the amount of your tax-free lump sum from between 30-35% down to 25%. I cannot understand why this restriction applies to retirement annuities, but that is obviously something which must be taken into account at the time of retirement – whether you feel that you need a larger tax-free lump sum, or whether your need for increased income is going to be greater with a reduced tax-free lump sum from a retirement annuity.

If you are *employed*, and on a pension scheme which does not have a very good history of pension increases in retirement, it may well be in your interest to apply to have your occupational pension scheme transferred into a personal pension plan prior to your occupational pension scheme retirement date. You will then be able to utilise the open market option which may be a better option for you for increased income at that time. However, much depends on the level of transfer value which is offered to you by your employer, and you need to weigh up which route will have the greater level of benefits for you. Factors which need to be taken into account include widows' and orphans' benefits, as well as life cover and other protection benefits which may be offered by your employer, which you may not be able to achieve through transferring your funds into a personal pension plan.

Have your retirement planner do this calculation for you, as it might mean a significant uplift in your future income benefits. This is particularly the case if you are no longer with a particular employer and your funds have merely accumulated in that employer's pension scheme. You will have considered this strategy during your retirement countdown phase in any event, but it does no harm to reinforce it at this time. Note that if you wish to transfer from your employer's fund to a personal pension plan or a buy-out bond, this process should begin at least within the last 12 months before you aim to retire, unless you have already left that particular company.

The correct utilisation of the open market option is an investment strategy which can significantly improve your income in retirement. When I formed the first annuity bureau in the United Kingdom, nearly 10 years ago, this was one of the uppermost thoughts in my mind. How would it be possible to take an existing situation and provide the best investment advice in respect of it? The major problem was that, although individually companies offered lower and higher annuity rates if you transferred your funds to any particular product provider, no one knew who they were and even if they did, it would take them months of work to ascertain which were the best at any one point in time. Today, there are sophisticated computer programmes around which will instantly give you the highest annuity rates on offer.

STRATEGY 105
Ensure that you have the correct investment profile if you have deferred taking your pension

---

Those who have elected the phased or income drawdown facility, thereby deferring the eventual taking of their annuities, still need to consider the correct investment strategy for their funds which remain within the pension fund.

Your investment risk profile, and the length of time which you are deferring the eventual taking of your retirement or pension benefits, will determine whether you should be invested in lower-risk fixed interest type securities or in higher-risk growth investments, such as equities or unit trusts, or whether you should be seeking more of a balanced portfolio which could deliver income.

Most people seeking a phased retirement programme, where you take an annuity and a lump sum at various stages in the retirement process, will no doubt be more growth oriented, hoping for the maximum value of fund build-up. Those merely seeking a drawdown of income from their pension fund, until such time as they must mature the fund (up to age 75) may well be seeking a combination of growth and income-producing assets. In any one year, you are restricted in how much income you may draw down out of your pension fund so that you do not deplete the capital unnecessarily and leave yourself in reduced circumstances when the eventual retirement date occurs. This restriction, where the government actuary has set minimum and maximum levels of income to be drawn down, is covered in Chapter 6 and Appendix 1.

STRATEGY 106
Make the correct annuity choice

In Chapter 6, you were given the full range of annuity options available. You will have noticed that these have changed over the years from being mere fixed income product providers to having a more flexible income choice. The more flexible choices provided through annuities which are, and remain, invested in unit-linked or with-profits funds, provide income which may fluctuate but should increase over time, compared to the more conventional annuity which provides a fixed rate of income for the rest of your life.

We always used to say that there is no growth in an annuity and that's the reason why you should leave your pension fund to grow for as long as possible. Today, this is no longer the case. One can have increasing income from an annuity merely because it enjoys increased investment performance. However, there is also a major disadvantage here in that income will fluctuate over the period, and only those who have sufficient resources to make up for any downside should attempt this route.

Because people do not know how long they are going to live, and because they also wish to provide income for their dependants, the natural inclination is to take an annuity with as many guarantees as possible. This can, in fact, be the worst possible option. The higher the level of guarantee which is taken, the lower the level of annuity income which will accrue to you. If the product provider has to guarantee annuity income over two lifetimes – for example, for you and for your spouse (a joint and survivor annuity) – then it will have to pay out an annuity in total for much longer than if you had merely taken it for yourself without providing in advance for your spouse. As a consequence, the annuity rate offered to you will be much lower.

The same is true in respect of choosing annuities which escalate at various levels – for example, at 3%, 5% or the general level of price increases (the RPI). The higher the level of escalation guaranteed, the lower the level of annuity rate offered to you. You may also wish to guarantee that, once the annuity becomes payable, should you die during the payment period, it will continue for another guaranteed period. If an annuity is guaranteed in this way, you can again expect a lower rate. Yet 95% of all people who take annuities also take as many guarantees as they can afford.

It was for this reason that the capital preservation option plan was developed which means that you do not need to take any guarantees – you merely select the highest open market option rate on a single life with a nil guarantee. Yet no one in his right mind would do this without any form of protection, so, in certain circumstances, you can preserve your capital by taking out an insurance policy on the value, or as much of the value as you choose, of the fund.

This option is the one which gives you the greatest level of flexibility. Some people will do it for a part of their fund – leaving the other part to enjoy guarantees or an annuity which escalates. It's all a matter of personal preference as to which route you decide to take.

The essential structure of the capital preservation option is such that it is designed to leave you no worse off than you would have been had you originally accepted the worst possible annuity arrangement. The worst possible income or annuity option is to choose a joint and survivor annuity which has a guarantee to pay a 100% spouse pension on your death. Escalating income and further guarantees to pay the annuity for a minimum period, say five years, will give you even less income. In Strategy 66 the worst income example given is £2,243 per year from a fund available of £60,000.

Compare this to a single life annuity with no guarantee (which offers greater flexibility later, if combined with the 'insuring the fund' concept) which given income of £8,340 from the same fund of £60,000.

The level of income received from that arrangement should be no worse than had you selected the highest level open market option single life with no guarantee *and* were paying the premiums on a fund protection policy. Whilst you are no worse off in income terms, the flexibility afforded to you in respect of investment strategy later on in retirement can be quite considerable – up to the extent of possibly doubling your income after, say, 10 years of retirement.

Let us take this concept a stage further. Assume that you had selected a joint and survivor guarantee annuity which would pay out for your lifetime as well as for that of your spouse, and your spouse died before you. You would still be locked into that lower annuity income for the rest of your life. However, had you selected the capital preservation option using the highest open market option single life with no guarantee, but with your fund protected, and you required additional income, and did not have any dependants to whom you would like to leave your full pension fund, you could merely cease paying your protected policy premiums and divert those to yourself as additional income.

Making the right annuity choice can be an irreversible decision. If you find, five years into retirement, that you have made the wrong choice, you are unfortunately stuck with it. Retirees at retirement date are therefore urged to seek the most flexible options available to them. These will usually be to defer the taking of their actual annuity for as long as possible, leaving the growth to accumulate within the fund, and then to decide whether annuity escalating income is required or not.

With regard to escalations in annuity income, the cross-over point for those who selected a level annuity (paying a fixed income for the rest of your life) and those selecting an escalating annuity at, say, 5% (where the annuity income starts at a lower level but escalates annually at 5% for the rest of your life), is at about the 10-year mark. In other words, you would have had lower income for the first 10 years and only after that period can you expect higher levels of income increasing *ad infinitum*.

Again, the investment decision will be made in respect of the size of your fund available. If you cannot make do on lower levels of income earlier on in the retirement process, you will probably be more inclined to take a level annuity. However, if you have funds surplus to your requirements, and your family has a history of longevity, you may wish to take the escalating option, or the with-profits or unitised annuity income option.

As you can see, this is a most complex area and to do full justice to it requires a thorough review of your present and future requirements as well as the amount of funds available to you.

One thing is certain, though: unless you have all the options laid out in front of you, you will never have enough information on which to make a correct choice. Retiring is all about choices. Proper planning with the correct options being decided on can make the difference between a happy and contented retirement or one which could be financially disastrous to you.

STRATEGY 107
Get yourself an experienced retirement planner – if only for a second opinion

---

You may have arrived at the actual retirement date all by yourself, making your own investment funding and management decisions, but unless you are a retirement expert, a lot of the good work which you put in previously may well be dissipated by making the wrong choices now.

It is, therefore, vital that you seek the advice and guidance of a recognised retirement planner, preferably someone who is a member of the Institute of Financial Planning or similar body. Where there are thousands of pounds at stake, be prepared to pay a reasonable fee to such a planner and let him have the financial planning stress of advising you properly. Having read this book, at least you will be able to keep your financial planner on his toes and you can even provide him with a shopping list. It is important that you have as much information as possible at your disposal, and are aware, for example, of the different types of options as well as investments available to you.

STRATEGY 108
Get maximum benefit from your employer

Your employer can help you in a number of ways, not only by contributing its share to your pension scheme. If you are self-employed or a partner, the general principles which follow would be equally applicable to yourself.

If at all possible, get your employer to arrange to have you sent on a retirement planning seminar which would preferably also include your spouse or partner. These types of seminars are held regularly and are given by various bodies. They are most useful, not only from a financial planning point of view, but also for telling you what to expect in retirement and how best to handle it.

Your employer could also initiate a retirement countdown planning programme which culminates in retirement investment and planning advice at the actual date of retirement. This is certainly in your employer's interest, as the last thing it wants is you knocking on its door afterwards to say that you never got enough, that the calculations were wrong and that more could have been done. In my own experience, there are very few benevolent employers around who even think about those who are going off on retirement – and yet, others actually employ people to make sure that their retired ex-employees are enjoying their retirement and are kept in touch.

If all you can expect after maybe 40 years of service is a gold watch and a goodbye party, then perhaps your employer is more the type to be concerned about those who stay rather than those who are going. Yet there are a significant number of ways in which your employer can assist you to have a happy and contented retirement. For example, if you have a company car this, in all likelihood, has to be handed back at the date of retirement. That would mean that, out of tax-free lump sum, you would have to replace this asset, as well as other corporate perks which you may have been enjoying.

It is entirely possible for your employer to provide you with a new motor vehicle a year or two before your retirement, which you may then take with you. Some employers have a continuation option on their death-in-service or group life scheme, which could also be most useful to you, particularly if you have become uninsurable or would be heavily loaded had you to replace group protection benefits from your employer with your own individually-costed arrangements. If the employer has a 'without medical evidence of health' continuation option on any of its protection schemes, then make sure you are aware of this. It could save you thousands of pounds in retirement.

For example, at least one of the income protection specialists for permanent health insurance (PHI) has in its scheme a benefit rider which allows you to continue to be protected, once in retirement, for frail care and residential care benefit. All of this is at a premium which stays exactly the same as when you first began paying it, or the company was paying it for you whilst you were in its employ.

It is possible that your employer does not offer a comprehensive package of employee benefits, such as critical illness cover which pays out a lump sum should you be diagnosed as having cancer, a stroke, heart problems or other dread diseases. However, these arrangements can be made at no additional cost to the employer, with tremendous savings for employees, merely by the employer agreeing to operate the scheme which is paid for by the employees on a group basis. This can even be arranged for you individually at a time when you are much younger, and set to continue at those younger-rated premiums when you are in your retirement years and when the possibilities of a dread disease occurring are much higher. For example, you have a 6-8 times greater chance of suffering a dread disease before the age of 65 than you have of dying in service before that age.

Consider what is more important to you as you get older. Your family commitments may well be less, much of your financial commitment will have been met in respect of liabilities, and you have excess salary as well as employee benefits which you don't really need – such as an expensive company car. If you feel you could make do with a cheaper car, for example, it would most certainly be in your interests for this 'employer money' to be diverted for your benefit into increased pension funding.

Let's face it – you work only to retire. It is therefore in your interests to make sure that you will be as comfortable and as financially secure as possible. Whilst you have 100% control over your own resources, getting your employer on your side to assist you, and, of course, other employees, could add to your wealth at retirement by up to 30% if not more. All of this can be accomplished at no real additional cost to your employer.

The same principles apply to the self-employed and partners in business seeking to maximise what the business can offer in order to increase their personal wealth as an investment strategy for retirement.

STRATEGY 109
At retirement date, cut costs and increase net disposable income

---

Purely from a marketing point of view, the retirement or 'grey' market has a powerful financial influence. It has been able to negotiate various discounts, solely as a result of spending power, for cheaper motor insurance, house insurance, travel and even food. Some of these benefits are offered from age 50, whether you are retired or not, and you should investigate to see whether they apply to you. Your strategy is to make sure that you can increase your net disposable income as much as possible and reduce your outgoings. A number of associations such as SAGA exist purely for this purpose.

It is an important time to consolidate your existing coverages and to get rid of obsolete ones, replacing them with more efficient ones if possible. You should, therefore, review all of your life insurances, critical illness coverages, car insurance, household insurance, travel expenditures and even mortgage commitments.

It is also the time to get rid of obsolete and outdated appliances, which might include washing machines, tumble dryers, television sets and so on. What you buy new now may have to last you for the rest of your life.

STRATEGY 110
Plan, using your home or other properties

As only 30% of people reaching actual retirement age will be financially secure, at least 70% of people will need to make up any shortfalls in funding and income requirements for the future through other means. For most people, this type of planning will concern how best to use the house or family home.

A number of plans are possible, whereby you may remain in your house whilst using the asset to provide you with an income or an annuity. Most of these plans involve the eventual sale of your house to repay the product provider who has provided you with this income opportunity and you will have to decide whether this is desirable, or whether you wish to leave an asset to your heirs. For example, it is possible to have an annuity raised against your fixed property whereby the interest, if you have taken a remortgage, is offsettable against your annuity income. At the date of your death, the property is sold, the loan provider is repaid and any balance is returned to your estate.

Whilst not ideal, you may let one or more rooms in your house and receive rental income to supplement your retirement income. Under Rent-a-Room Relief in the 1997/98 tax year £4,250 can be taken as rental income tax free.

STRATEGY 111
If you are retiring abroad, take professional advice

Which country you are retiring to determines the level and type of advice you will require in connection with your investments and pension income. Your investment strategy at the date of retirement will need to be properly considered, so as to be most tax efficient. This is a very broad area to cover and you are urged to take professional investment and tax advice before you consider any of your options. For example, once you emigrate, if you were deferring capital gains tax through reinvestment relief, the deferral period will end and you will immediately become liable for capital gains tax on that asset being sheltered. This may not be something you had bargained for.

Also, you may decide to retire to a holiday home in a foreign country and then, after a number of years, you may wish to return to the United Kingdom. It is important that you receive a proper level of advice in order to cope with these and other contingencies. Medical and travel insurance is usually a vital component of these plans.

STRATEGY 112
Investing for income or capital growth

At the *actual date of retirement,* once you have considered your options, your investments and pension schemes will require decisions to be made to provide you with adequate levels of income and access to capital.

If you are investing for income or capital growth, these are the most common investments, depending upon your risk preference.

Investment	Level of risk	Income	Growth	Tax relief
Current account	lower	yes	no	no
Offshore current account	lower	yes	no	no
90-day call account	lower	yes	no	no
Fixed deposits	lower	yes	no	no
TESSAs	lower	yes	loyalty bonus only	tax-free income

Investment	Level of risk	Income	Growth	Tax relief
Other bank instruments	lower	yes	no	no
Guaranteed income bonds	low/medium	yes	no	no
Corporate bonds	(possible capital risk) high/medium	yes	no (capital may fall)	no
Corporate PEPs	high	yes	yes	no
Treasury bonds	low	yes	possible	no
Government, other bonds	low/medium	yes	possible	no

Note that capital may fluctuate up and down with *any* bond

Investment	Level of risk	Income	Growth	Tax relief
Offshore bonds	medium/high	yes	yes	no
Endowment policy	medium	no	yes	no
Personal Equity Plan (PEP)	medium/high	no	yes	grows tax-free
Unit trusts	medium/high	yes	yes	no
Investment trusts	medium/high	yes	yes	no
Enterprise Investment Scheme	higher	dividends	yes	yes
Unquoted non-qualifying companies	very high	dividends	yes	no
Venture capital trusts	higher	dividends (tax-free)	yes	yes (20%)
EIS fund	higher	dividends	yes	yes (20%)
Alternative Investment Market (AIM)	higher	dividends	yes	no (unless EIS company)
Qualifying unquoted company for CGT reinvest-ment relief	higher	dividends	yes	yes (40%)
Share portfolio	high	dividends	yes	no
Enterprise Zone Trust (EZT)	high	yes	yes	yes (100%)
Pension fund contribution (self-invested pension plan or other type)	low	no	yes (tax-free)	yes (40%)
Fixed property	medium	rents	yes	no
Employee benefits and share schemes	low	no	possible	yes on some
Hard investments (work of art etc)	high	no	yes	no

At the actual date of retirement, you will therefore have investments already in place, and new investments to be considered for your tax-free lump sums, as well as the investment strategy for your underlying pension schemes if you are deferring the taking of a pension until a later date.

There are many factors to be taken into account and retirees are also faced with many dilemmas. These include having to accept fixed incomes with no hope of increasing them; lower pensions for spouses or no pensions at all for spouses; the fear of having inadequate income brought about by longer periods of retirement and the fear of outliving your capital; no further opportunities for lump sums; effects of inflation; post-retirement debts; fear of financial insecurity; an inadequate State pension; the high cost of guarantees on annuities; the loss of a pension fund on death, and many other aspects. If you have limited capital resources at the actual retirement date, you will also be more inclined to accept a cautious investment philosophy, meaning that your funds under investment will not grow to the same extent as if you had been more adventurous. The cautious approach underlies your main concern for the protection and preservation of your capital, which is understandable.

Weighing up all of these aspects will assist you in developing your investment strategy for the future.

Those with surplus funds can adopt a more relaxed attitude and can be more adventurous in their investment approach. However, this should not be to the detriment of their funds, and they should seek to maintain their capital as well as to grow it as effectively as possible.

THE INVESTMENT PROCESS IN RETIREMENT

Most of your investment decisions will have been taken at the actual retirement date and your strategies in retirement will be more concerned with ensuring that your retirement income remains adequate and that your investments are properly managed.

As most investments are made at retirement date, with fewer capital sums coming up for reinvestment after retirement, financial advisers generally ignore the post-retirement market for new business. Yet, it is in retirement that the retiree requires an ongoing level of retirement advice to make sure that investments already made do not become obsolete over time and are performing as well as can be expected.

STRATEGY 113
Regularly review your investment portfolio in retirement

Regular reviews and monitoring of your investment portfolio and sources of income are an important feature in the retirement process once you have already retired. Some retirees merely make the investments and leave them to continue under their own steam. Others regularly review their portfolios, to take account of changes in tax legislation, new types of investments coming into the marketplace, or changes in their circumstances. You should ensure that you do this – when you are in retirement you will have more time to spend on these aspects.

STRATEGY 114
Change your investment strategy if your circumstances change

Whilst in retirement you will again have many different choices and investment strategies depending upon your circumstances and your requirements for yourself and your dependants and heirs. It is at this time that you begin to consolidate your estate planning – for example, making gifts of capital to children or grandchildren, looking at inheritance tax saving devices and planning for the possibility of selling your house and moving into residential care. This latter aspect is covered in Chapter 10.

Having spent your lifetime building up your investments and your pension funds, as well as accumulating diverse assets, the last thing you want to do is pay away over 40% of their value in inheritance taxes through not having planned the final phase of your investment strategy in retirement.

It is therefore important to consolidate your estate planning with your retirement planning and to make sure you have an effective will (and this includes your spouse) which is up-to-date. You may also wish to take tax planning advice at this stage, in order to attain the optimum position for both yourself and your heirs.

Purely from an investment point of view, you should utilise as many of your tax allowances as possible, bearing in mind that your post-retirement income may not be as high as that which you were earning pre-retirement. Many investors at this time will be topping up their personal equity plans annually, as well as making investments into national savings plans and building society investments such as TESSAs. Many will also be building society and bank investors, where those institutions have changed from being a mutual to a company. There may also be privatisation and other issues with which to contend, and there will most certainly be investment decisions to make in these areas.

Some investors at this stage decide that they would rather opt out of the intensive investment management process and want to consolidate their investments by selling off individual shares, for example, and having the proceeds reinvested into unit trusts or bonds. Again, there is a considerable amount of investment planning to be undertaken if you are in that position. This may well coincide with your other objectives in respect of equalising your estates to reduce the future incidence of inheritance taxes, passing investments to your spouse or partner in order to create lower tax-paying situations, and planning funding for going into residential care.

Your investment strategy may change significantly as your age increases. You may decide that now is the time to use more of your capital in order to supplement the income which you already have, and this is often the case if you have no dependants. Those with dependants may well do exactly the opposite in order to meet these need requirements. The investment process is therefore an ongoing situation which requires constant monitoring.

INVESTING FOR DEPENDANTS AND HEIRS

Should your dependants inherit from you, then the investment cycle will begin again. Some investments may be kept as they are, but the chances are that significant changes will be made.

You may leave a surviving spouse, partner or children, and planning has to be done for this eventuality. This planning will actually have started prior to reaching your retirement date and your dependants can expect either a pension arising from your own funds, or various lump sums from your investments, insurance policy pay-outs, and bequeathed assets.

Often inheriting dependants are not as financially astute as you may have been, and will require further professional investment advice on how to treat assets and capital for reinvestment purposes. Again, this would depend on their circumstances at the time. For example, a surviving spouse in advanced years would, in all likelihood, expect a most cautious approach as far as reinvestments are concerned, to provide sufficient income, as well as some capital growth, whereas children investing will start at the beginning of the investment cycle and will, in all likelihood, be more equity or higher growth oriented.

If you set up trusts in your will, the investment clauses must be sufficiently wide to ensure that your financial planners are able to undertake the correct type of investments. Often, investments in trust end up in low growth investment areas, which are difficult to change, because of the rules relating to trustees investing into 'safer' investments. However, you can give wider investment powers to your trustees in your will.

The investment planning process never ends. It just becomes someone else's concern. New investors in the decision-making process will have different investment criteria, as well as investment strategies, and may well appoint new investment managers and financial planners for themselves. This is only to be expected. However, what you leave and how you leave it will be all-important for those who come after you and your planning will dictate how successfully you provide for others.

In all my years of advising on financial planning issues, I have yet to meet a widow who says that she received too much. However, I have met plenty of people who say they haven't had enough!

Key points summary

- Investment planning strategies for retirement are given for each of the stages from the accumulation phase during one's working life, up to the actual act of retirement, and then into retirement. Strategies are also given for dependants and heirs.
- Whilst the accumulation and contribution phase dictates retirement investment strategy, the real choices occur at actual retirement date. These are important and often irreversible, and strategies are given in respect of investing lump sums, taking annuities or leaving funds to accumulate in deferred pension arrangements. Consideration is also given to how an employer may assist the retiree and what other decisions to take around lifestyle planning requirements.

- The importance of monitoring and reviewing investments continues during retirement and reinvestments may have to be made as investment risk changes. Considerations are also given to increasing income in retirement and what sorts of investments produce income as well as capital growth.
- Investment planning continues for dependants after the death of the retiree, when the whole portfolio should be reconsidered, depending on the need requirements of spouses, children and other heirs.

Action plan

- Revisit your retirement objectives. These are as follows:

  _____

  _____

  _____

- The following are my most likely retirement choices:
  - to take a lump sum and a reduced pension ❏
  - to take a full pension with no lump sum ❏
  - to preserve my capital as long as possible ❏
  - my most likely annuity options are:
    - an annuity for myself and my spouse with guarantees ❏
    - a single life annuity with no guarantee and fund protection ❏
    - drawing down income from my pension scheme and deferring the annuity until age 75 ❏
    - phasing my retirement income and capital to meet my requirements ❏
  - I wish to preserve assets for my dependants *or* ❏
  - I do not wish to preserve assets for my dependants, but would rather use them for myself ❏
  - I will be my own financial expert *or* ❏
  - I will need a good retirement planner to assist me ❏
  - can my employer help? ❏
  - what further assistance do I need for the best retirement plan? ❏

- Draw up your own investment risk profile like those in strategies 77 and 112

INVESTMENT RISK PROFILE

Investment	Level of risk	Income/capital growth

- Draw up your own investment process like that in strategy 112

THE INVESTMENT PROCESS

Investment	Amount to invest

CHAPTER 8

Retirement Strategies For Your Business and Family

Old age is the most unexpected of all the things that happen to a man.
***Diary in Exile*, Leon Trotsky (1879-1940)**
An income is what you can't live without or within.
Unknown Author

Objective: Wealth creation from the business, including strategies to pay dividends, bonuses, make pension contributions, employ your spouse and family with suitable tax-efficient business exit options

Most workers and business owners will derive the vast proportion of their wealth from their employment or work, as well as employee benefits linked to health, protection of family, disability, pensions and so on. For business owners the business itself is also a source of potential wealth if it can be sold and the value realised. Some people will be fortunate enough to supplement their business or employee wealth accumulation through inheritances or private means, but most will rely on their employment or business to do so.

The more salary paid to you, the higher the tax burden. In addition, employers and employees alike pay national insurance contributions, which is another form of taxation. If savings can be made by mitigating taxes and then creating wealth through pre-tax or lower tax investments strategies (as opposed to merely investing after tax), then surely this is a sensible way to proceed.

Companies

Companies making profits have a number of choices on how to benefit employees. They can do one or more of the following:

- Pay a dividend from profits after tax.
- Pay a bonus from taxable income before corporation tax, itself a business expense reducing tax payable.
- Make a pension contribution for an employee or director which reduces corporate tax liabilities.
- Make a benefits-in-kind payment which may or may not be taxable in the employee's hands.
- Set up group scheme benefits arrangements which have cheaper premiums – often up to 15 times less than if made individually from after-tax employee money.
- Provide the means for shares to be purchased from the company by employees by, for example, making gifts or loans to an employee trust (where capital payments are tax deductible to the company).
- Enter into a variety of profit-sharing schemes and, although it is being wound down by the government, enter into profit-related pay (PRP) schemes.

Some of the above will apply only to certain employees (for example, only shareholders can receive dividends), whereas other arrangements are more generally applicable, such as bonus payments and NIC-avoiding benefits in kind.

Partnerships

Partnerships can do one or more of the following to benefit partners and employees alike:

- Profit share arrangements. Partnership employees cannot have a stake in the business, unless they are partners. A 'Phantom Share Scheme' for employees can be set up, however, which will have the same effect.
- Paying bonuses or effecting bonus diversion schemes.

- Making maximum pension contributions (personal pensions and SSAS schemes for partners), final salary, money purchase, group personal pensions and hybrid schemes for employees.
- Make benefits-in-kind payments to employees; set up group scheme arrangements for cheaper employee benefits, as well as profit-related pay before the scheme ends.

Sole traders

By definition, a sole trader *is* the business. The sole trader can only contribute to a personal pension for the self-employed, and will lean more towards personal financial planning, maximising personal investments, as well as deductible expenditures incurred in the business which are allowable.

STRATEGY 115
Is it better to take a dividend, bonus or pension contribution and bonus? Select the best option for your circumstances

---

Whilst the example used below is for high-paid executives, the principles underlying the strategic planning apply to any company situation, and for any number of employees.

Example:
Assume that a business is prepared to pay £100,000 from profits for the benefit of an employee, who is also a shareholder, and paying income tax at the highest rate.

The amount of dividends available for distribution is decided by the corporation tax rate of the business. The higher the rate, the lower the level of dividends available.

In the summary below, the difference between a dividend and bonus payment is shown for a higher rate (40%) taxpayer in 1997/98. It includes the dividend less the amount of the tax credit available of 20%.

Corporation tax rate	Bonus route net of tax	Dividend route (net)	% change over bonus
21%	£59,106	£59,250	+£144 or 0.0024%
31%	£59,106	£51,750	-£7,356 (-12.45%)
33.5%	£59,106	£49,875	-£9,231 (-15.62%)

From the above table, it is marginally more tax efficient to only take a dividend if a higher-rated taxpayer, where the company's corporation tax rate is *lowest*. It is a better net effect to take the bonus and pay tax on it at higher levels of corporation tax. (Note that if the amounts involved are much less, and if a basic rate taxpayer, then the advice on which route to take may be different.)

Assuming the company will still spend £100,000, there is yet a better way, and that route includes a bonus plus pension contribution.

Bonus (after employer's NIC of £4,545)	£45,455
Less 40% tax	(£18,182)
Available cash	£27,273+
Pension contribution	£50,000
Net position for executive	£77, 273

Corporation tax rate	Bonus route net of tax £	Dividend route net £	% change	Pension contribution £50,000 + bonus £27,273	Value after 10 years at 12% p.a.
21%	59,106	59,250	0.0024%	-	£1m
31%	59,106	51,750	-12.45%	-	£1.25m
33.5%	59,106	49,875	-15.62%	-	-
Either	27,273	-	30,74%	£77,273	£1,525,000

Using the pension/bonus route would increase the net worth of the executive immediately by over 30% and this position is maintained if the net amounts were invested for 10 years with a return of, say, 12%.

> ## STRATEGY 116
> ## Don't only do it once – assess the position each year for maximum tax-free fund building

The company is no worse off – it will spend the £100,000 on the executive (less company NIC at 10%). By using the best strategies year after year, even the smallest business can obtain the optimum wealth accumulation for its employees.

> ## STRATEGY 117
> ## Bonus diversions can be made for optimum tax efficiency. Examine every possibility

Employers can quite legitimately save National Insurance contributions by making investments or providing benefits in kind for employees. Some of these will save the employer NIC, currently at 10%. For example, a *pre-retirement benefit scheme* (in trust for employees) is presently available which has no National Insurance contributions payable, is not a taxable benefit in kind, payments are deductible to the business, there is no P11D or PAYE to pay, no corporation tax, no inheritance tax and no capital gains tax payable.

No doubt this tasty morsel will eventually be closed down by the authorities, but it has already successfully withstood a number of attacks and is backed as effective by senior counsel's opinion. It is certainly worth consideration by employers with £100,000 or more available to spend on executives.

> ## STRATEGY 118
> ## Do a loan account redemption scheme to make your money grow for you

There is no growth on your loan account money in the business. You may have loaned the business £50,000 ten years ago. It is still only worth £50,000, deflated for inflation in value.

You may or may not have received any interest on your money

over the years and, if you have, it may not have been very much.
Replace your money with bank money or other people's money
(OPM). Get your cash out now and invest it.

£50,000 invested in PEPs, pension contributions, VCTs, unit
and investment trusts, OEICSs, endowments or offshore growth
bonds will be worth £150,000 – 200,000 in 10 years' time, if not
more.

STRATEGY 119
Use your spouse in the business to create big savings

Using your spouse or partner in the business can not only save
you thousands of pounds, but also help to boost pension and
retirement funding significantly. Imagine having the monthly
housekeeping tax deductible!

The Inland Revenue will want to be sure that your spouse or
partner actually does do some work in the business (and, in fact,
that *any* family member used in this way does) and you should
give your spouse an employment contract if an employee, or
include the arrangement in a partnership agreement, if a partner.

Spouses will have many skills to assist you, or your employer,
and can effectively deal with secretarial duties, typing, marketing,
reception, conference organising, filing, research, accompanying
you on business trips as an assistant, bookkeeping, customer
dealing and general management duties.

Salaries paid to spouses are *tax deductible* to the business.
Bringing the spouse into the equation creates huge tax savings. A
benefit is not a benefit unless you can use it. Everyone has certain
basic allowances which are often unutilised. The personal
allowance is £4,045 in the 1997/98 tax year if under age 65, and
rises to £5,400 at age 75+. This allowance means that the first
£4,045 anyone earns is *not taxable*.

Lower incomes also incur less tax. *You* could be paying tax at
40%, but your spouse could pay only at 20% or 23%. If you could
reduce your tax band to 23% then the saving of tax payable is a
whopping 17%.

Now, let's at least make the housekeeping tax deductible.

Example:
To pay his spouse monthly housekeeping of £1,000 per month
actually costs Patrick Mason £20,000 a year. He first earns the
£20,000, pays tax on it, then gives Alison the remaining £12,000
at £1,000 a month. Patrick earns £40,000 a year: Alison earns
nothing, but could assist in the business.

1. PATRICK GIVES ALISON HOUSEKEEPING

Present position (97/98)	Patrick £	Alison £
Drawings/salary	40,000	0
Personal allowance	(4045)	0
Taxable amount	**32,955**	-
Tax	(9822)	0
Net after tax	**30,178**	-
Housekeeping		12,000
Balance (disposable income)	**18,178**	**12,000**

2. PATRICK EMPLOYS ALISON

Employs Alison	Patrick £	Alison £
Drawings/salary	28,000	12,000
Personal allowance	(4,045)	(4,045)
Taxable amount	**23,955**	**7,955**
Tax	(5,386)	(1,706)
Net after tax	**22,614**	**10,294**
Housekeeping adjustment	(1,706)	1,706
Balance (disposable income)	**20,908**	**12,000**

Total income tax savings   }
Increase in disposable income   }   £2,730

Employer NIC will be the same, but Alison will pay £1,042 more
in NIC leaving £1,688 in savings. This is still £140 per month for
a savings or pension plan!

STRATEGY 120
Give your spouse or partner a tax deductible pension plan

In the above example, Alison could contribute at least 17.5% of £7,955 to a personal pension plan – £116 per month – further reducing the tax payable by £320. (Patrick would have to further adjust the housekeeping by £1,072 a year to enable the pension to be paid, as well as the full amount for housekeeping expenditures.) However, Alison would now have a pension plan in her own right.

Alternatively, Alison could be employed and earn up to £3,223 p.a. tax and NI free. The business could pension these tax-free earnings. The level of pension funding is substantial, based on that salary – up to more than *twice* the salary level.

The business can fund for employees (of companies, partnerships and sole traders) an Executive Pension Plan which is most effective for working spouses.

Married male or female retiring at age 60, salary £3,223 p.a.

Present age	Annual current funding allowed	% of salary
25	£838	26%
40	£1,644	51%
50	£3,577	111%
55	£7,445	231%

STRATEGY 121
If the business is a partnership, make your spouse a partner

If you give your spouse a share in the partnership profits, this would be treated as earned income and would give entitlement to a personal plan.

The maximum contributions to a personal pension plan (1997/98) are:

Age at 6 April 1998	Contributions as a % of net relevant earnings
35 or under	17.5%
36-45	20%
46-50	25%
51-55	30%
56-60	35%
61 and over	40%

For example, if you are age 52, with pensionable earnings of £15,000 p.a., you can contribute 30% (£4,500) a year into a tax deductible pension plan. Your strategy would be to establish if you would be better off as an employee or as a partner as pension funding limits are approximately double under an executive personal pension at this age. An executive personal pension plan is only available to employees, not partners. Do the sums to establish which route is most affordable and best for you.

Using your spouse in the partnership could double your retirement exit reliefs if you sold the business.

Employing your spouse or bringing your spouse into the business as a partner is a most cost-effective way of transferring income, capital and benefits from the business. This may have appeal for those in retirement, considering a new business venture.

STRATEGY 122
Use the business for maximum pension contributions

This can be accomplished only if the employer is firmly on the side of the employee. It may be appropriate for the business to entertain a total benefit review to see exactly what can be done for executives and other employees in the business.

In fact, the business need not be put to any additional cost if it cannot afford it. It can co-operate with the employee through a *salary sacrifice* scheme which would save income tax as well as National Insurance contributions by diverting previous salary into pension funding.

If salary sacrifice is used, then make sure it does not affect the value of other benefits. Reducing salary may reduce taxation (by having a pre-tax investment benefit into pension funding) but it could *also reduce* the employer pensions based on a multiple of salary. The rules of the pension fund may include 'notional earnings' taking into account a salary sacrifice.

Some employers have a *flexible benefit programme* allowing you to take a lesser value company car, for example, and put more into pension benefits as you get older.

Funding issues are dealt with in Chapter 3.

Business owners should consider withdrawing director *loan accounts* from the business and use these for tax deductible additional voluntary pension contributions, replacing working capital with bank finance or share capital introduced by ESOT (Employee Share Owner Trust) arrangements.

It is an unfortunate fact that most directors, employees, partners – and even sole traders – are nowhere near their maximum funding levels for pension purposes. Using the business to maximum fund their pension schemes, is the best way not only to build personal wealth, but also to ensure a better retirement.

After all, generous tax reliefs on funding enable approved pension arrangements to be built up partially funded by the Inland Revenue because of the tax deductibility of pension contributions.

Business exit options

STRATEGY 123
Plan to exit from the business as tax-effectively as possible

---

Business owners will have a number of options, depending on their circumstances.

Those who have been in business for at least 10 years and are over age 50 will qualify for maximum retirement reliefs from capital gains tax (1997/98):

The first £250,000 is exempt
The next £750,000 is 50% exempt
Annual CGT exemption is £6,500

Example:
Assume Helen Benson sells her shares in the business for £500,000. She is age 60 and has owned them for 15 years, thus qualifying for retirement reliefs.

Sale proceeds	£500,000
Purchase price including indexation	(£60,000)
Balance	**£440,000**
Less relief at 100% on £250,000 and 50% on	
(£440,000-£250,000) £95,000	(£345,000)
Chargeable gain	£95,000
Less annual exemption	£6,500
CGT payable at 40% on	£88,000
=	**£35,400**

This tax must either be paid, or the net chargeable gain reinvested into a qualifying company or investment to defer the tax payable.

STRATEGY 124
If a partner, make sure your capital account is repayable on favourable terms

---

A partner's capital account reflects imbedded value in the partnership. It is more or less the loan account (tax has been paid on accumulating it) of the partner to the business, and belongs to him or her.

The problem is, however, that the business may need this capital for working capital purposes and may not be in a position to repay it all at once. Whether retirement or death is the issue, that capital account may only come out in instalments over many years.

It is important to have a *fund*, so that capital accounts can be paid out. Many partnerships merely insist that individual partners maximum fund their *own pensions* and treat that as value received (effectively leaving capital to accrue to the other partners).

Beware, though, that on death, without any formal agreements in place, heirs have an immediate call for *cash* from the partnership and for value. *Get those partnership agreements in place*.

It is possible to have the partnership pay out an unfunded unapproved pension fund to the retiring partner (see Chapter 3), which may substitute for the inability to access capital accounts at the appropriate time.

STRATEGY 125
Ensure that there is a market for your shares on retirement

According to the Federation of Small Businesses, the biggest single query to them from business owners is how best to exit the business. Smaller businesses or minority share holdings may be extremely difficult to sell.

Start thinking *now* about a likely exit route: selling to surviving shareholders and partners, management and staff, third parties, other businesses, employee trusts, or whatever. Some people merely wind the business down and take a liquidation dividend. Others plan to exit via the AIM or Stock Exchange.

This is an area which must be properly planned well in advance *and* as part of the retirement countdown process.

STRATEGY 126
Take the company car with you on retirement

Avoid buying a new car out of your pension cash lump sum. Persuade the business to let you keep your company car and plan for a new one a year or so before retirement.

The business could gift the car to you, or sell it to you at a written-down (for depreciation) value. It could loan you the money to buy it (writing off the loan) or provide you with the car in retirement at its expense. As you are no longer an employee, there should be no benefits-in-kind tax to pay.

If the business donates the asset to you as a gift, you may be liable for CGT, but remember that you have an annual exemption of £6,500 in 1997/98.

STRATEGY 127
Get expert advice to plan your business exit properly

Only some of the main exit routes are mentioned here. Different circumstances will mean different advice – don't leave it too late. It may be quite an exercise getting rid of the business, and it may take years to get it ready, *and* to obtain the best price for it.

Some will exit the business 100% – other may want to take a less active part. Whatever the process, *plan, plan, plan*!

Key points summary

- Retirement strategies are discussed for business owners and employees.
- The best ways to take capital out of the business and to increase income tax effectively are shown.
- Using the spouse in the business – not only for big tax savings but also to get the housekeeping tax deductible! – and building up spouse pensions are considered.
- Partnership issues on leaving the business, along with retirement reliefs for *all* business owners, are discussed.
- Importance of maximum pension funding and bonus diversions for best effect are shown.
- Business exit options at retirement date and retirement reliefs are given.

Action plan

- Read *Wealth Strategies for Your Business*, published by Century, for over 500 strategies on how to build wealth through your business.
- Establish if the business is in a position to help you build wealth in a tax-efficient manner. Make a list of those things which you have and do not have but would like to have. Make the approach.
- Are you selecting the best options to take profits from the business? Can you do better? Can the business pay a bonus or make a pension contribution for you, or must it always only pay dividends? Find out which is the best route.
- Do you have loan account money in the business? Is it working

for you? Would it be preferable to replace it from alternative sources, allowing you to invest elsewhere? Examine all the options.

- Consider taking your spouse or partner into the business to enjoy more disposable income through lower taxes and to give your spouse or partner a pension of their own.
- How do you intend to exit from the business and when? Do you have a plan in place? Which option would you prefer? Are you working towards making it reality? Draw up an exit plan.
- If you need it, get expert advice. It may save you thousands of pounds in the long run.

CHAPTER 9

Preserving Your Retirement Capital

I advise you to carry on living, if only to infuriate those who pay your annuity.
Voltaire, to a sick friend

Objective: To preserve your retirement capital and income-producing assets and not to lose them on death. To keep more of what you have in the event of living longer than expected

The biggest fear for anyone approaching retirement is outliving your income and capital, or not having enough to live on in your retirement years. The second biggest fear is losing what you have already accumulated when you die.

If your retirement capital has been built up through the traditional route of pension funding, then at some point in the future you will have to *give up control* of a substantial part of your pension fund (at least two-thirds) to what is known as an annuity provider, usually a life office – leaving you in control of only one-third, your tax-free lump sum. This would be the case whether you were employed or self-employed.

What happens is this. The amount of your pension fund designated to provide you with monthly income (the pension or annuity) is invested by the life office or pension provider. Various factors are taken into account, such as your age, health, mortality (how long you are expected to live) and the amount available for investment.

If you select a joint and survivor annuity, then when you die, your spouse or partner will enjoy a pension or annuity for the rest of his or her life. If you, or you and your spouse or partner, outlive the income provided by the annuity or pensions provider, then you are ahead of the game. If you die before you have had maximum employment of your funds, then the pensions provider is ahead.

This system is quite rightly seen to be iniquitous, and has recently provoked a flood of letters to *The Times* amongst others. The excuse generally used by the product providers is that they are more or less entering into a bet or wager with you *and* all the other retirees on how long you will live.

Annuity providers are not concerned with your personal welfare or that of your family. They are only concerned with actuarial calculations and other factors on how long they will have to pay out for. They will also be the first to point out that you cannot have it both ways – enjoying retirement income beyond your actuarially-determined life expectancy *and* picking up any fund surpluses.

Not so. In some countries, such as South Africa, some annuity fund surpluses can be returned to heirs and dependants. In the UK it merely translates as profiteering on a grand scale. Now the life offices will tell you one thing, whereas the possibilities on what happens to your retirement capital may well be something else. In his reply to a reader's question in the *Times* debate on what happens to annuitants' capital on death, the managing director of the Equitable Life (also an actuary) made the point that the retirement funds of those who die early support the retirement income of those who live longer than expected, and eventually one must expect the capital to be exhausted. He particularly stated that the present return on gilts was *less* than the amount paid out to annuitants, implying annuity income was made up from a return on capital as well as other investment interest.

What he did not mention was that the charges made by the annuity provider also come from this annuity investment, as well as commissions to intermediaries, and that the true investment position may in fact be different. Whilst a large proportion of annuitants' capital is invested in gilts (to provide a fixed income), a considerable portion is invested in the equity market. Where gilts may return, say, 7-8% per annum, equity returns could be 50% or more.

In addition, the *trends* for annuities indicate that they are becoming more personalised and more accurately determined.

Impaired lives, smokers, workers in certain occupations, obese people, those terminally ill and so on can all now benefit from enhanced annuity rates. Sometimes these are 30% more (for smokers) or 500% more (terminally ill) than the original quotation. The individualisation of annuities will mean more accurate capital allocation to provide the annuity and less reliance on pooling. It is simply ludicrous for the annuity providers to hide behind the pooling concept (some will lose, some will win) any longer. Annuity provision is big business for them – sometimes at the expense of the annuitant.

Using up your fund

Example:
After taking the tax-free cash portion, John has a pension fund of £200,000 left to provide an annuity income. He is aged 65 now, and is expected to live to age 78. He is married to Mary and has selected a reduced pension for her, guaranteed for five years. Mary dies before him.

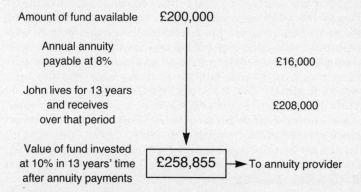

Amount of fund available	£200,000
Annual annuity payable at 8%	£16,000
John lives for 13 years and receives over that period	£208,000
Value of fund invested at 10% in 13 years' time after annuity payments	£258,855 → To annuity provider

Whichever way you look at it, the annuity provider will be investing your fund, not merely paying you back your own capital. Therefore, no matter when you die, there will *always* be a proportion of your capital left which provided the basis for these pension payments in the first place.

Example:
If John had taken his annuity and lived for five years, then died, Mary would have received a 50% reduced pension for her lifetime.

If she lives for another 10 years, then the pension is as follows:

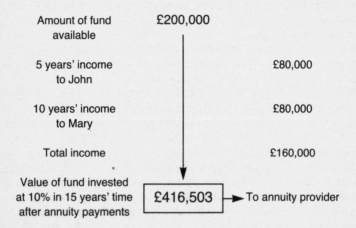

Amount of fund available	£200,000	
5 years' income to John		£80,000
10 years' income to Mary		£80,000
Total income		£160,000
Value of fund invested at 10% in 15 years' time after annuity payments	£416,503	➤ To annuity provider

If your pension is received from an employer, for example, under a final salary scheme, the actuarial determinations if annuities are used are more or less the same.

Your fund portion would still represent a capital base provided from contributions made by the employer and employee jointly. For larger, self-administered pension funds, providing for 'final salary schemes' for example, it is the employer, or a combination of the employer and an annuity provider who provides your pension or annuity. Any surpluses then accrue to your *employer's* fund or the annuity provider if you die.

Where employers pay pensions, a variety of income streams may be used for pensions in payment and it is more difficult to lay claim to any surpluses. Such surpluses are usually used for the benefit of later retirees through pension increases or lower contributions by the company.

Employer pension payments

- Fund capital is used to purchase an annuity; *and/or*
- Pensions are paid from investment income; *and/or*
- Pensions are paid from cashing in investments; *and/or*
- Pensions are paid from income (like salaries); *and/or*
- Pensions are paid from company retained reserves.

Much has to do with liquidity within the pension fund itself, as to which route the employer will opt for. However, apart from the very large final salary schemes, most employer pension schemes are administered by life offices, which arrange annuities to meet pensions in payment.

It is obviously going to be much easier for *annuitants* to fight for future pension surpluses, than for employees receiving pensions from employers which have diverse income-streaming.

What strategies can then be employed by the prospective retiree to preserve retirement capital for future generations? This is a major question, which has led many to query whether they should be going into pension funding in the traditional way at all.

No one wants to build up a pension fund, then have limited use of it, only to lose the bulk of his or her capital on death. The *best solution* would be for annuity providers to declare a surplus fund amount on death (after their costs and charges, obviously) to be payable to a nominated beneficiary. Public pressure could force this issue.

However, in the absence of such a possibility at present, the following strategies could be employed.

STRATEGY 128
Always take the maximum tax-free cash available and invest it yourself

---

At least you will have *control* over some of your funds. The tax-free cash lump sum can be invested to provide for income and capital growth and is available for your heirs.

STRATEGY 129
Check with the annuity provider as to what happens to your fund surplus on death in retirement

---

You never know – if enough potential annuitants make this request, maybe we will see a major shift in attitude by the annuity providers, and even some employers with their own schemes.

STRATEGY 130
Insure your pension fund

It is possible to insure your pension fund, free of evidence of health at retirement. You can do it earlier when it is cheaper to do so. By doing this, your flexibility in retirement is *greatly* increased. You may even get better rates if your health is underwritten. If you get *worse* insurance premium rates, then it is possible to get an even *higher* annuity rate.

Anyone who has insured the capital value or expected value of his or her pension fund can then select the best annuity option at retirement. The worst annuity option is to take a joint life and survivor annuity. This will pay out for your lifetime and for your spouse's. However, the *annuity rate* offered will be the *lowest* because the annuity provider must hedge its bets to pay out for two lifetimes. It's even worse if guarantees are taken up. If your spouse unfortunately dies before you do, you will *still* be locked into that same joint and survivor, two lifetimes rate. The same level of original income will be received by you, irrespective of the fact that the annuity provider planned to pay it out for the two lifetimes.

By insuring your pension fund capital value, you are now free to select the *best annuity rate* possible, a single life with no guarantee. Highest annuity rates are offered for this option, as well as maximum flexibility.

If you die, the full value of your pension fund pays out for use by dependants and heirs. The proceeds are tax-free and sheltered from inheritance tax.

STRATEGY 131
Don't wait until retirement to insure your fund

The earlier the better. If selecting this option, you must choose a whole of life policy. Term cover may be cheaper, but doesn't always pay out when you need it.

Before retirement you may have to go for a medical examination, but it's worth it. This is also an ideal opportunity to give your heirs and dependants a *bigger* pension fund than you may have enjoyed.

In any event, adequate life cover is an integral part of personal financial planning. For most people, though, the need for greater levels of life cover reduces as they get older, in this case (insuring your fund) it needs to be adequate. There are three types of life coverage suitable for this arrangement, depending upon your purchasing power. Term cover, maximum cover whole of life, and standard cover whole of life.

Term cover

Very few insurers will produce term coverages which are more or less 'open-ended'. After all, the cover must be for your *lifetime* and must end at some date before you die. However, it is possible to obtain 50-year terms and effecting this type of cover from age 50 onwards would usually enable you to beat the odds on outliving it. If you do live beyond age 100, and you took pension benefits from age 50, you will definitely be ahead of the game in respect of benefits already received, in any event.

Term cover provides a constant regular premium for *level* term with an exact coverage pay-out. There is no investment element, and premiums should be cheaper.

LEVEL TERM ASSURANCE: 50 YEARS £100,000 COVER

Age next birthday	Male		Female		Cost as a % of cover p.a.	
	Premium per month £	Premium p.a. £	Premium per month £	Premium p.a. £	Male	Female
51	117.5	1,410	73.64	884	1.4	0.8
56	162.39	1,949	102.4	1,229	1.9	1.2
61	226.51	2,718	140.68	1,688	2.7	1.6
66	241.39	3,497	177.93	2,135	3.4	2.1
71	338.26	4,059	207.79	2,493	4	2.5

Non smoker rates, normal health

Maximum cover whole of life

This is a whole of life policy which provides the maximum level of life cover. There is a negligible investment element. Whilst it is the cheapest form of whole of life cover, there is a danger that premiums could be reviewed (usually every 10 years) and could increase (or the sum assured could decrease). This type of cover is not really suitable to cover your pension fund, unless you can afford the premiums at older ages.

Age next birthday	Premiums per month		Expected fund value cover
	Females	Males	
30	20*	20*	£100,000
40	20*	20*	£100,000
50	32.08	52.28	£100,000
55	50.48	86.28	£100,000
60	79.88	139.48	£100,000
65	123.68	216.08	£100,000
70	191.38	328.68	£100,000

minimum premiums quoted

Whole of life standard cover

Whilst standard cover premium costs are more expensive than maximum cover premium costs, this is because more goes into the investment element of the policy contract. As a result, there is no need for a premium review to maintain the cost of cover in later years.

More positively, this type of contract can be used to build up a *second* lump sum in retirement. This could be most useful if your retirement circumstances change radically, and will give you the flexibility to vastly *increase* your *income* in retirement.

Example:
Assume that John and Carol are married, and John retires at age 60, whilst Carol is age 55. John selects the best open market option single annuity with no guarantee for the best possible highest rate. To protect his original pension fund on death, John takes out a standard cover whole of life policy to pay out the full value of his original pension fund for Carol's benefit as lump sum in cash. The standard cover policy insuring his fund value has a surrender value (cash value) after 10 years of £14,800.

Assume Carol predeceases John after 10 years in retirement.
John still has the value of highest annuity rate available with the single life no guarantee annuity. If he *had taken* a joint and survivorship annuity with guarantees, at the lowest annuity rate, he would be *locked into* that level of income for the rest of his life.

Now, at least he has flexibility. If he needs more income, he can cease paying the premiums (this diverts more income to him), and surrender the life policy to provide *additional income* when invested, or merely gift the cash to his heirs.

In the table below, the cash value of his policy after 10 years is £14,800 and this would provide an income of £1,480 p.a. if invested at 10%.

Assume John predeceases Carol after 10 years in retirement.
Carol receives the full value, in trust, of the original pension fund, because the life policy pays out. She is now 10 years older and will receive a *higher* annuity rate for a voluntary purchase annuity. This type of annuity is also more tax-efficient (some of it comes to you tax-free), meaning even higher income is possible.

Carol has significantly *increased* her income in retirement. If she and John had originally opted for the lower income joint and survivor annuity with guarantees, Carol may instead have been receiving an income of up to 50% *less* after John's death. Instead, she has *more than doubled* what she would have had, 10 years after retirement!

Age next birthday	Female	Premiums per month Value after 10 years	Male	Value after 10 years*	Expected pension fund value cover
50	91.52	6,810	123.45	8,920	£100,000
55	132.03	9,510	176.51	11,900	£100,000
60	187.45	12,500	246.08	14,800	£100,000
65	256.33	15,400	327.89	16,200	£100,000
70	339.20	16,400	419.04	12,700	£100,000

* Growth rates assumed at 10%. These are not to be taken as quotations

---

STRATEGY 132
If employed, you can also insure your pension fund

You have a number of options to consider here. Your employer can help you with maximum group life cover through the business. As present, you can have four times *final* salary, which may equate to as much as eighteen times *annual* salary.

Make sure, though, that the business has arranged a *continuation option* on your group life or death-in-service benefits plan. This enables you to continue with your life cover once you have left the business. It is pointless to plan your strategy via the business, only to fail at the final hurdle.

Continuation cover is at the *rate for age* at retirement, and you pay the premiums on the cover. It may therefore ultimately be cheaper to effect your own pension preservation life cover at your age *now*, and get the business to pay for it.

At retirement, you may well be better off transferring from your employer's fund to a personal pension arrangement (arrange this at least a year before retirement), if the options for higher annuity income and total fund preservation are greater than merely accepting the employer's pension. Look at all aspects, including future pension increases.

Some individuals arrange their affairs in such a way that they benefit from employer pension increases, as well as pension fund preservation.

STRATEGY 133
Unless you have selected the insured option, delay taking your pension fund as long as possible

---

Unless you're on a company scheme with set retirement dates, those with retirement annuities, personal pensions and SSAS arrangements can defer taking their full pension benefits until age 75 at present.

This means that the underlying pension fund can remain invested as long as possible, providing more growth for greater income later. Income can be withdrawn from the pension fund within limits, but an annuity must be taken by age 75 at the latest.

Income drawdown and phased retirement are retirement planning options for income and capital which serve to extend the eventual retirement date, allowing the underlying capital to accumulate, but should be planned in conjunction with pension fund preservation. See Chapter 6 for details on how to pass the fund to dependants when income drawdown (taxed) or phased retirement (tax-free) occurs.

STRATEGY 134
Retain maximum control of capital and income for as long as possible

---

The problem with taking an annuity is that, once taken, it becomes totally inflexible. It cannot be changed or even rearranged for better income later, if your circumstances change. In addition, there is usually no growth in an annuity – only in the underlying pension fund.

Your optimum strategy is to obtain the highest level of income for as long as possible, whilst ensuring preservation and growth of your capital.

Whilst you will have maximum control of your tax-free cash for investment purposes, the same is not true for the balance of your pension fund.

Until such time as the products change and the law changes, allowing unqualified access to retirement income and capital, it is up to the retiree to plan as best as possible in a most restrictive environment.

It is legally possible in certain instances to transfer the trustees of your self-administered pension scheme (SSAS) to an offshore tax haven. To date, many millions of pounds' worth of pension assets have been transferred in this way, allowing virtually unlimited access to capital and control of funds. Inland Revenue approval must first be obtained for transfers of this nature.

STRATEGY 135
If fully funded, make use of a FURBS for controlled capital preservation

---

A FURBS is a 'Funded Unapproved Retirement Benefit Scheme'. It is commonly used as a top-up to approved pension funding. The employer makes contributions to the fund, receiving tax relief as a business expense, and employees are taxed on the contributions which are treated as a benefit in kind for tax purposes. Commonly, National Insurance contributions are saved by the employer, whilst the payments made count as salary, thus increasing the limits for normal pension funding.

Investment income is taxable, but at the basic rate. Income received is taxable, but lump sum benefits are not. Most benefits are paid as a lump sum and then a voluntary annuity, which is tax-effective, is purchased. Retirement from a FURBS usually mirrors your normal retirement date. The FURBS can purchase and hold unconventional assets, such as the purchase of a holiday cottage, or company shares.

On retirement, an annuity may be taken, as well as capital, which can then be invested elsewhere with full control.

See Chapter 8 for other areas where the business may assist you with funding your plan.

Key points summary

Various strategies are given to preserve pension fund capital and to ensure its use for heirs and dependants, without necessarily losing it to the pension or annuity provider. These include:

- Ways to preserve and pass on pension fund capital.
- Ways of protecting pension fund capital on death.
- Insuring your pension fund.
- Keeping control.
- Benefits of delaying the final maturity of your fund whilst still enjoying its income.
- Measures to be considered for SSAS and FURBS arrangements.
- Obtaining maximum flexibility whilst considering capital preservation options.

Action plan

1. If capital preservation is important, examine all the appropriate options. Much will depend on which route you take as to which preservation options are most suitable.
2. Tax and inheritance tax planning are also important and should be undertaken.

CHAPTER 10

Long-term Care in Retirement

No one thinks of winter when the grass is green.
A St. Helena Lullaby, **Rudyard Kipling (1865-1936)**

Objective: To preserve your estate for your heirs if you have to go into care or a residential home nearing the end of your retirement

The transition from normal retirement to retirement *with* long-term care is usually a subtle one. Whatever the reasons for physical or mental disability occurring, if someone is unable to look after herself or himself satisfactorily, then proper care and attention is required from, usually, a nursing home or 'Care in the Community' provided in one's own home.

What should be borne in mind is that the costs of long-term care could financially cripple a retiree, leaving his dependants destitute, using up income and assets to such an extent that nothing is left available for his heirs – and I mean nothing.

In fact, if you spend more than six weeks in hospital, your old age pension and other benefits can be diverted in order to pay for the cost of your care. After that indignity (which may leave nothing to pay for the running costs of your home, such as gas, electricity, telephone expenses which still exist whilst you are in hospital), the costs of then going into a nursing home average £800-£1,000 per month – without frail care facilities.

Your only chance of becoming a burden on the State is if you have assets worth not more than £16,000 and if your income can be means-tested. Otherwise, assets must be sold (including your house unless a dependant is living in it) or investment encashed to cover your costs of care.

Whole inheritances can be consumed in this way, often leaving dependants and heirs without a penny. The main thrust of the complex legislation surrounding long-term care and nursing home costs is that you use up your assets and income first in providing for it, and only then does the Department of Social Security (the DSS) and your local authority take over the responsibility of caring for you.

Irrespective of the value of your assets, you may expect at least the following:

State old age pension   £62.45 per week in 1997/98
Attendance allowance   £32.40–£48.50 per week (if you qualify)

There may be other benefits available to you, such as disability allowances, but these are usually very small.

The 'Catch 22' situation is that only the more impoverished will benefit from State and local authority help, whilst the wealthy will pay their own way, maintaining their capital and income streams. The broad mass of the population will be caught in between – not having enough to pay the full costs, they must use up their capital until such time as it is exhausted, and only then will other agencies take on the burden.

It is therefore *vital* that, in order to conserve your estate, you have enough income or income-producing capital to meet *rising* costs at the last stages of life.

The seriousness of this problem is underlined by the fact that many people, themselves approaching retirement, have the additional burden of having to provide and care for an elderly relative. Without adequate lifetime pension and investment funding, savings and long-term care plans become prohibitively more expensive the older you get.

Whilst thinking about retirement is a far-removed possibility for younger working people, considering long-term care is even more remote. Most people only wake up to the fact that it may happen when their circumstances dictate. By then it is often *too late* to do any realistic planning. That is the reason why long-term care provision should be an extension of normal retirement provision and its adequacy.

After all, you will be already retired (unless you suffer a pre-retirement disability or lasting illness) when the aspect of long-term care becomes a possibility, and this prospect could seriously damage your wealth.

It is estimated that the financial cost of care for an 80-year-old is up to 10 times higher than that of someone 20 years younger. The message is clear – as you get older, you will need *more* money, not less.

The present legal position is that elderly persons with savings of at least £10,000 and assets – excluding the value of the house – exceeding £16,000, must contribute towards residential care costs, and receive no assistance at all. The house (unless a dependant lives in it) and all other assets will have to go to provide for this care, until only the £10,000 is left.

Residential care costs could be in excess of £20,000 a year, and over 40,000 people lose their homes *each year* to provide for this.

Whilst long-term care insurance and investment policies are available, the wealthy don't need them and the poor can't afford them. Those in the middle must decide if the expense is worth it. The only alternatives are to remain as poor as possible and let the State pick up the tab, or to ensure sufficient capital-producing income is available as well as pensions to pay the increasing costs expected.

At the same time, you need to consider all the legal means available to protect your assets and capital base for your heirs. Legally, this can be done. Practically, it *must* be done. Astute ongoing financial advice will look at exempted assets.

STRATEGY 136
If you wish to shift the care payment burden to the State and local authorities, get your capital into exempt areas

---

Whilst the local authority will take into account capital and income in assessing how much you pay, there are ways of retaining assets, and income from those assets, so that they do not fall into the assessment trap.

Capital includes property, shares and money, but not capital held by a discretionary trust. Some income and capital is exempt by law and this may cause a reallocation of assets by the individual to take advantage of the legislation.

Beware the 'sting in the tail', though. Local authorities have the power to treat you as *notionally* possessing capital, which you have *at any time in the past* deprived yourself of to reduce the amount of your liability to pay for residential care fees. However, they must prove you did this to avoid paying fees. If you have a right to funds but fail to claim, it could also be treated as a deprivation of capital.

However, the local authority cannot seize your assets if they have been transferred – even if you did so to avoid liability for fees. Their only power lies in reclaiming assets transferred up to six months before you entered what is known as Part III accommodation.

Therefore, plan carefully to avoid the six-month period, and, preferably, at least five years before entering care to avoid the possibility of a local authority bankrupting you to get at your assets. This is unlikely, but remains a remote possibility.

What, then, are exempt assets and income? Capital assets to be disregarded (Schedule 4 of the National Assistance {Assessment of Resources} Regulation 1992) include:

- The *surrender* value of a life policy (but not the proceeds of maturity or surrender).
- The *value* of one dwelling under certain circumstances. For example, if a spouse or partner lives there, or a qualifying relative, or if the move to residential care is a temporary one.
- *Proceeds* of sale of any premises formerly occupied.
- Future interest in property other than in certain land and premises.
- Gifts in kind from a charity.
- Personal possessions, including works of art.
- Certain business assets.
- Certain rights which have not yet crystallised as cash but would have a value to a third party.
- Capital not in your name. However, transfers of assets to a spouse or partner may be caught at a later date if he or she goes into care. Only your share of a joint bank account can be included.

There are a number of other capital disregard provisions, but the above are the main ones.

Certain income is also excluded from the calculation as being exempt. This includes income from certain disregarded capital assets; payments under the Income Support Regulations; income under an annuity; from personal injury trusts and a life interest or a life rent; earnings from outside the United Kingdom; tax payable, income from charitable or voluntary bodies paid as expenses and other payments; up to 50% of your occupational pension if not residing with your spouse, or maintaining her; payments by third parties towards your living costs; any income in kind; certain payments from insurance policies; council tax benefits; income support for housing costs – and a whole host of other exemptions.

The main *planning areas* appear to be around the following for the protection of capital and future income streams:

- Investments in qualifying *life assurance policies*. These can be held in trust.
- *Transfers of assets* to heirs, preferably up to five years before considering the possibility of long-term care. Future heirs pay your costs. Six months is the earliest, possibly eighteen months to two years before will convince the authorities not to invoke the notional capital rule.
- Planning around the *house* or main dwelling, using appropriate relatives or selling up, or using a trust.
- Planning with *trusts* to protect assets for the benefit of future generations. If properly constructed, assets and income could be put beyond the reach of local authorities, both as actual or notional capital. If the costs of care run to £20,000 or £30,000 a year, the 1% annual charge on trust assets for administration will save the individual up to £100,000 in 3-4 years alone. It's worth investigating this with your financial adviser.
- Trusts are also useful for inheritance tax planning. Therefore:

STRATEGY 137

If the possibility of going into long-term care is identified, and you wish to keep costs down whilst protecting capital and assets, consider a trust

---

The reasons for this action are given above and should be part of your retirement financing programme.

Even if you can afford residential and long-term care costs, no one knows what course of action the government may take in the future to put your assets at risk again.

The long-term care debate continues as you read this. The State has already shifted much of the responsibility for caring for the aged from the DSS to local authorities, themselves overburdened and under-funded. It is the intention of the State to make individuals more accountable for their own retirement *and* long-term care provisions – but few people can do this. The stress of losing your house, investments and income from pensions and other sources is almost too much to bear for the elderly who paid National Insurance contributions during their working lives and saved hard for retirement.

Future generations will also lose out. Inheritances will disappear to the local authorities in increasing costs. Long-term care for their parents will ultimately be paid for by future generations, either through increased National Insurance contributions or indirectly through losing assets usually passing from parents to children.

It is therefore an important aspect of retirement planning and financing that not only the early retirement years are considered, but also the later ones.

STRATEGY 138
Consider a long-term care investment

It is now possible to invest a lump sum into a plan from which premiums are taken to cover the cost of long-term care or accommodation. You may keep as much control of the underlying investment as you feel is necessary, or use part or the whole of your investment if this is required.

The intention is to insure against the risk of long-term care, whilst still keeping your capital assets intact, and not having to bother with trying to beat the DSS and local authorities means-testing. This also gives a far wider choice of home as you are not reliant on the local authority placing you into care, but can make your own arrangements.

Key points summary

- Long-term care or residential care is an important – and, for most of the elderly, a *definite* – part of post-retirement planning.
- Whilst wealthier retirees can afford increasing costs in later retirement, and the poor are provided for, the broad mass of elderly citizens could be impoverished through escalating costs.
- Planning is important to preserve and protect assets and capital, as well as income flows in retirement – already 40,000 people lose their houses each year to the local authorities to pay for care.
- Future generations will not inherit in the same way as before, unless estate preservation programmes are considered.
- It's inevitable – you work, retire, possibly go into residential housing or care, and then you die. How well you do it is what counts!

Action plan

- Is going into care or a residential home after retirement a possibility? _____
- Do you wish to keep assets for heirs, or will you use these to pay for care costs? _____
- Can you support care costs alone, or will the DSS/local authority have to help?_____
- Do your estate planning now depending upon your future expectations and objectives.

Retirement and Pensions Overview

One cannot divorce pensions from politics. The over-55 age group is today the most powerful lobby in the United Kingdom. Not only are more people retiring earlier, they are also living longer. This means that their money has to go further than ever before. The past decade has seen a fundamental shift in attitude by the government to create a greater environment of self-reliance, as it realises that it will not be able to support the burgeoning pensions bill incumbent on the State in the future. In fact, we have already seen the beginnings of State abrogation, as the government winds down its state earnings related pension scheme (SERPS). History will show that this is possibly one of the biggest experimental failures of government when a whole generation of pension fund savers were bribed to opt out of the state system into guaranteed minimum pension plans issued by the private sector. This was also the root cause which led to allegations and proven pensions misselling in the eighties and nineties, and the reinstatement of individuals into occupational pension schemes and also opting back into SERPS. With the new Labour government, we have a rejection of Tory privatisation, and a re-emphasis on the basic State pension, coupled with the idea of a compulsory second pension scheme if you are not in one already.

Over the years we have had a mass of new regulations designed to protect those in pension schemes. The fact of the matter is that there is no State actuarially funded pension scheme. There is no State pension fund. The workers pay in National Insurance contributions on a Friday, and the pensioners draw out the same amount every Monday. It is obvious that any future increases in State pensions will only come from an ever-increasing burden of higher National Insurance contributions from those in employment for those in retirement.

The man in the street is caught by two gross misconceptions. The first if that the State will provide. The second is that the employer will provide adequate pension funding for the employee. Whilst this may be true to a limited extent in both instances, the true facts of the matter are that employers, ever on the look-out to save costs, are reducing their commitments to employee pension funding, and even radically changing the nature of their schemes to accomplish this.

The self-employed are not immune to this malaise either. Unable to conceive that adequate pension funding must start as early as possible within a working lifetime, most only wake up to the harsh reality within 10 years or less of retirement. Most of their funding is also inadequate.

Whilst the State is trying to shift its retirement pension obligations more and more to the private sector, the private sector in turn is hampered by repressive legislation which does not allow for adequate and flexible retirement funding and planning.

Examples in this area are legion. The whole retirement funding process is tax-based and not benefit-based. Ask anyone who retires how much retirement income he or she would need. Usually the answer is, 'I need 100% of what I was earning, increasing for inflation.' Yet the maximum that the individual is allowed to fund for under present legislation is two-thirds of final salary, and that only after 40 years of unbroken service. So we have in place legislation which determines how much can be funded for in respect of building up your pension fund. We also have legislation in respect of the amount which may be contributed towards a pension scheme. This is also tax-based. If you do not have the relevant taxable earnings then, plainly speaking, you may not commence any approved pension funding. This effectively cuts out more than a third of the population receiving income from their spouses, or who have independent means – for example, from investments which they would like to put towards approved pension funding. This applies to both occupational pension scheme funding by individual employees, as well as personal pension funding by the self-employed or directors.

Not only are you limited in contributing on your way in – as well as in how much pension you can take when you retire – but, should you make the mistake of possibly *over-funding* your pension scheme, you are then hit with harsh tax penalties and what is left after payment of these penalties is returned to you. The basic rule is this: your contributions which qualify will be tax deductible to you. These contributions will accumulate within a tax-free environment within your pension scheme. When retirement date arrives, with most schemes you can select a lump sum to be paid to you, some of which is tax-free. Any pension or annuity received by you will be taxable.

Your pension scheme is your best investment for tax-free growth, whilst the fund is in existence, so long as the fund is approved. If you were funding for adequate retirement benefits on a *benefit-funding basis* (as opposed to a tax-funding basis), then there is a strong view for a more flexible retirement funding basis, even within the existing tax legislation. This could be accomplished by allowing you to fund what you like, receiving some tax deductibility on your contributions which qualify, and allowing your surplus contributions, which are not tax deductible, to accumulate tax-free within the pension scheme. At retirement date, these non-tax deductible contributions will merely increase the size of your tax-free lump sum or give you a larger pension scheme from which to draw a pension or an annuity which will be taxable. A more flexible approach could also be achieved through changing the definition of what constitutes 'net relevant earnings' for retirement funding contribution purposes.

Finally, there is distrust of the pension providers and life offices used for pension funding when a pensioner dies. In the United Kingdom at present, the balance of the pensioner's fund passes to the insurer, or pension provider, and not to the heirs or nominated beneficiaries of the deceased. This is seen as profiteering on the part of the life offices, and in at least one country insurers are now returning these surpluses to the heirs.

The above overview shows an inflexible, highly complicated approach to pension and retirement funding in the United Kingdom. If the State wishes to liberalise its retirement funding ideas, instead of merely tweaking the existing system, then it has plenty of scope to achieve this. It could certainly simplify the entire process. There will never be a significant shift towards massive build-up of private or personal retirement funding until such time as the entire culture changes. As we now have transparency with pensions costs and charges (where the consumer is made aware of what he is letting himself in for), it is surely also the time to address the whole pensions and retirement funding environment, whilst opening the door to greater pension funding and retirement possibilities.

Until then, the strategies in this book are designed to enable you to maximise your personal objectives, and to do the best for yourself within the existing framework. Using a qualified retirement planner, able to offer independent financial advice, to assist you through the process of retirement planning will be essential for most people contemplating these important lifetime decisions.

Of all the decisions you ever make, those for your retirement are the most important.

APPENDIX 1 (SEE STRATEGY 68)

MAXIMUM AND MINIMUM INCOME WITHDRAWALS

Male age attained	Value of fund[1] after tax-free cash	Maximum withdrawal[2] p.a.	Minimum withdrawal[3] p.a.
60	£100,000	£9,500	£3,325
65	£100,000	£10,600	£3,710
70	£100,000	£12,100	£4,236
74	£100,000	£13,800	£4,830

Female age attained	Value of fund[1] after tax-free cash	Maximum withdrawal[2] p.a.	Minimum withdrawal[3] p.a.
60	£100,000	£8,700	£3,045
65	£100,000	£9,600	£3,360
70	£100,000	£10,800	£3,780
74	£100,000	£12,200	£4,270

1. Non-protected rights portion.
2. Based on government actuary's determination and a gross redemption yield rounded to 7% (30 July 1997). The calculation is only valid for a three year period and must be redone every three years.
3. 35% of the maximum figure for three years, before recalculation.

An annuity must be purchased outright *before* age 75 is attained. If the member dies during the deferral period, then a surviving spouse or dependant may make income withdrawals until age 75 or, if earlier, the 75th anniversary of the member's date of birth.

Bibliography

Brown, Rosemary *Good Retirement Guide 1997*, Kogan Page

Burrows, W. C. *Annuity Direct, Gold Service,* Annuity Direct, 27 Paul Street, London EC2A 4JU

Burrows, W. C. 'Impaired Life Annuities' in *Money Management,* July 1996

Burrows, W. C. 'Serious Considerations' in *Planned Savings Commercial Union Supplement,* 1996

Chandler, Beverly *Financial Care for Your Elderly Relatives,* 1st edn, Longman

Foreman, A. *Allied Dunbar Tax Handbook 1996–97,* 1996, Pitman

Galea, Claire 'How Income Drawdown Works' in *Planned Savings Commercial Union Supplement,* 1996

Granger, A.A. *Annuities and Retirement Planning; Retirement Planning 1* (seminar notes and guides), IFP Training, Harrogate

Granger, Tony *Wealth Strategies for Your Business,* 1996, Century Business

Heritage, John *Residential Care Fees: Don't Let Them Grab the House,* 4th edn, September 1996, Acorn Press

Homer, Arnold and Burrows, Rita *Tolley's Tax Guide 1996–97,* 14th edn, Tolley Publishing

Jordaan, Johannes and Heystek, Magnus *How to Plan for a Happy Retirement,* 1993, Helderberg

Levene, Tony *Daily Telegraph – Planning for Retirement,* 1986, Daily Telegraph

Wicks and Philip *The Financial Advisers' Handbook,* 1996, Gee

Wright, Diana *Sunday Times Personal Finance Guide to Your Retirement,* 1996, HarperCollins

Pension Facts (Various), London and Manchester Pensions Ltd

Pensions Pocket Book 1997, NTL Publications Ltd, in association with Bacon and Woodrow

Retirement Income Options, Save and Prosper Group

Simply SIPPS, Winterthur Life

The Which? Guide to an Active Retirement, 1st edn, 1993, Consumers' Association

RETIRED INVESTORS' GUIDE

Contact Private Client Department
The Independent Financial
   Partnership Limited
Windsor Court
Clarence Drive
Harrogate HG1 2PE
Tel: 01423 523311
Fax: 01423 569501

WEALTH STRATEGIES FOR YOUR BUSINESS

Published by Century
Author: Tony Granger
Available from book shops (£13.99)
or from The Independent Financial
Partnership Limited (as above).

Contains over 500 strategies to
increase profits and reduce costs.
Aimed at small to medium
businesses, this book has already
had a major impact.

RETIREMENT PLANNING SERVICES AND SEMINARS

For retirement advice, contact your
independent financial adviser, or the
author, Tony Granger, and his
advisory team on 01423 523311.

RETIREMENT PLANNING SOFTWARE

Tailor-made interactive software is
being designed to assist with
financing your retirement, making
maximum contributions, retirement
choices and options, and to show
you your benefits at retirement, as
well as how to become your own
retirement expert. There are also
software options for ' what if?'
scenarios to assist with planning. To
register for information, fax Wealth
Strategies Business Publications on
01743 360827.

Index